Presented To

Presented By

Date

Jesus said,
"Beware! Don't be
greedy for what
you don't have.
Real life is not
measured by how
much we own."
LUKE 12:15 NLT

JESUS
speaks to
TEENS

Whoever walks with
the wise becomes wise,
but the companion of
fools suffers harm.

JESUS
Speaks to
TEENS

NOT YOUR Ordinary MEDITATIONS ON THE WORDS OF JESUS

❖ BETHANY HOUSE
Minneapolis, Minnesota

Jesus Speaks to Teens
Copyright © 2004 by GRQ Ink, Inc.
Franklin, Tennessee 37067

Published by Bethany House Publishers
11400 Hampshire Avenue South
Bloomington, Minnesota 55438
www.bethanyhouse.com

Bethany House Publishers is a Division of Baker Book House Company, Grand Rapids, Michigan.

Scripture quotations noted CEV are taken from THE CONTEMPORARY ENGLISH VERSION. © 1991 by the American Bible Society. Used by permission.

Scripture quotations noted GNT are taken from GOOD NEWS TRANSLATION, SECOND EDITION, Copyright © 1992 by the American Bible Society. Used by permission. All rights reserved.

Scripture quotations noted NIRV are taken from the HOLY BIBLE, NEW INTERNATIONAL READER'S VERSION™, Copyright © 1995, 1996, 1998 by International Bible Society. Used by permission of Zondervan Publishing House. All rights reserved.

Scripture quotations noted TLB are taken from *The Living Bible* copyright © 1971. Used by permission of Tyndale House Publishers, Inc., Wheaton, Illinois 60189. All rights reserved.

Scripture quotations noted THE MESSAGE are taken from *THE MESSAGE: The New Testament, Psalms and Proverbs.* Copyright © 1993, 1994, 1995 by Eugene H. Peterson. All rights reserved.

Scripture quotations noted NASB are taken from the NEW AMERICAN STANDARD BIBLE® Copyright © 1960, 1962, 1963–1968, 1971, 1973–1975, 1977, 1995 by the Lockman Foundation. Used by permission.

Scripture quotations noted NCV are taken from The Holy Bible, New Century Version, copyright © 1987, 1988, 1991 by Word Publishing, Dallas, Texas.

Scripture quotations noted NIV are taken from the *Holy Bible: New International Version* (North American Edition)®. Copyright © 1973–1978, 1984, by the International Bible Society. Used by permission of Zondervan. All rights reserved.

Scripture quotations noted NKJV are taken from THE NEW KING JAMES VERSION. Copyright © 1979, 1980, 1982, Thomas Nelson, Inc., Publishers.

Scripture quotation noted NLT are taken from the *Holy Bible*, New Living Translation, copyright © 1996. Used by permission of Tyndale House Publishers, Inc., Wheaton, Illinois 60189. All rights reserved.

Scripture quotations noted NRSV are taken from the New Revised Standard Version of the Bible, copyright © 1989 by the Division of Christian Education of the National Council of the Churches of Christ in the USA. Used by permission. All rights reserved.

Library of Congress Control Number 2003018463.
Jesus Speaks to Teens, ISBN 0-7642-2866-8

Compiler and Editor: Lila Empson
Manuscript written by Vicki J. Kuyper
Design: Garborg Design Works

04 05 06   4 3 2 1

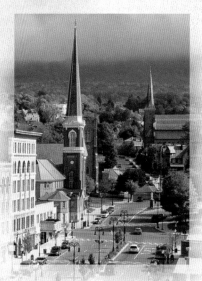

It's in Christ that
we find out who we
are and what we
are living for.

EPHESIANS 1:11a THE MESSAGE

Contents

Introduction

Put yourself in the disciples' sandals for just a moment. Picture Jesus speaking directly to you.

The truth is, Jesus' words have as much power to change your life today as they did the lives of those listening two thousand years ago. The words Jesus spoke, as recorded in the Gospels, are still fresh today. They speak about peer pressure, teamwork, and living life to the extreme. Jesus' words speak to you.

Jesus Speaks to Teens will give you insight into the story behind those words. You'll step back into Jesus' day to experience the culture, audience, and emotions that played a big part in the lessons and parables Jesus shared. Then you'll be challenged to take what you've learned and apply it to your everyday life at home, at school, or hanging out with your friends. Additional Bible verses and quotations will help move you one step further, drawing you up close and personal to the Savior who calls you by name.

Let Jesus' words speak to you.

It's an Inside Job

Jesus said, "If you walk around with your nose in the air, you're going to end up flat on your face, but if you're content to be simply yourself, you will become more than yourself."
Luke 18:14b THE MESSAGE

THE STORY BEHIND WHAT JESUS SAID

Jesus was with a group of people who put others down while building themselves up. Jesus taught them a lesson through a story about a Pharisee and a tax collector. In Jesus' day, the Pharisees were the in crowd of Jewish society. Tax collectors, on the other hand, were the local losers. Society looked down on them and ridiculed them.

The prayers of the two men revealed what they were really like. While the Pharisee played to the crowds, making sure everyone saw him pray, the tax collector hid his face, begging God's forgiveness. In Jesus' eyes, the attitude of the tax collector was greater than that of the Pharisee, for God could work in his humble heart to make him a man worthy of honor.

12

REFLECTIONS ON THE WORDS OF JESUS

Appearances can be deceiving. Suppose someone tries to sell you a hot-looking car that you'd love to buy. If the mechanic who checks out the engine says the car probably won't make it across town without breaking down, what good is a great paint job?

The same holds true for people. It's what's on the inside that really counts. If you're doing all the right things for all the wrong reasons—so others will think you're someone worth looking up to—what you're doing isn't really worthy of honor. It's just a great-looking paint job.

Everyone has the potential to be someone great. How you relate to God—not your talent, income, or even your good deeds—is what makes your life count. A proud heart craves the applause of others. A humble heart longs to do whatever brings honor to God, regardless of whether anyone is watching.

ONE FINAL THOUGHT

The bigger you are in your own eyes, the less room there is for God to work in your heart.

TIMELESS WISDOM FOR EVERYDAY LIVING

It's an Inside Job

Christ, the master of humility, reveals his truth only to the humble, and hides himself from the proud. Vincent Terrer

Whichever one of you is the most humble is the greatest.
Luke 9:48b CEV

For those who would learn God's ways, humility is the first thing, humility is the second, humility is the third.
Saint Augustine of Hippo

God sends no one away empty except those who are full of themselves.
Dwight L. Moody

Reverence for the LORD is an education in itself. You must be humble before you can ever receive honors.
Proverbs 15:33 GNT

Do not think of yourselves more highly than you should. Instead, be modest in your thinking, and judge yourself according to the amount of faith that God has given you. Romans 12:3 GNT

Be humble in the presence of God's mighty power, and he will honor you when the time comes.
1 Peter 5:6 CEV

The reason why God is so great a Lover of humility is because He is the great Lover of truth. Now humility is nothing but truth, while pride is nothing but lying.
Saint Vincent de Paul

If you are looking for an example of humility, look at the cross.
Saint Thomas Aquinas

15

Finding Your Focus

Jesus said, "I am leaving you with a gift—peace of mind and heart. And the peace I give isn't like the peace the world gives. So don't be troubled or afraid."

JOHN 14:27 NLT

THE STORY BEHIND WHAT JESUS SAID

The very last meal Jesus spent with his disciples was a dinner to celebrate the Jewish feast of the Passover. Knowing he would die soon, Jesus took extra care in choosing the last words he would share with the twelve men who were closest to him.

Jesus promised these friends and followers a priceless gift, the gift of peace. In the next few days, Jesus would be arrested, tried, beaten, nailed to a cross, and would die. The disciples themselves would be facing questions, grief, fear, and possible persecution. Obviously, the peace Jesus promised wouldn't be found in external circumstances. It would be found in spite of them, inside the disciples' own minds and hearts.

REFLECTIONS ON THE WORDS OF JESUS

Inside your yearbook, you expect to find photos of your friends. If instead you found pictures of their books, cars, feet, and leftover lunch trays you'd be pretty disappointed with the photographers. They would have focused on the wrong things, filling your yearbook with unimportant stuff.

Focusing on what's most important not only makes a better yearbook but also makes a more peaceful mind and heart. Whether you're facing a major disappointment or a personal tragedy, there are times when it feels like everything is falling apart—but that doesn't mean that you have to.

God knows what today holds for you, and you needn't face it alone. He has promised you the same gift Jesus promised his disciples: peace. When you change your focus, looking at how big God's love for you is instead of how big the problems that surround you are, you'll find peace, even when your life is anything but peaceful.

ONE FINAL THOUGHT

When the world feels as though it's falling to pieces around you, God offers you a place of peace inside you.

TIMELESS WISDOM FOR EVERYDAY LIVING

Finding Your Focus

A heart at peace gives life to the body.

Proverbs 14:30a NIV

May God bless you with his special favor and wonderful peace as you come to know Jesus, our God and Lord, better and better.

2 Peter 1:2 NLT

You had no hope, and you did not know God. But, now in Christ Jesus, you who were far away from God are brought near through the blood of Christ's death. Christ himself is our peace.

Ephesians 2:12b–14a NCV

A Christian is an oak flourishing in winter.

Thomas Traherne

Let the peace that Christ gives control your thinking, because you were all called together in one body to have peace.

Colossians 3:15a NCV

You, LORD, give perfect peace to those who keep their purpose firm and put their trust in you. Trust in the LORD forever; he will always protect us. Isaiah 26:3–4 GNT

Keep your heart in peace; let nothing in this world disturb it: everything has an end.
Saint John of the Cross

Let us fix our gaze on the Father and Creator of the whole universe, and cling to his splendid and superlative gifts of peace.

Saint Clement of Rome

We should have great peace if we did not busy ourselves with what others say and do. Thomas à Kempis

True to Your Word

Jesus said, "I say to you, do not swear at all. . . . But let your 'Yes' be 'Yes,' and your 'No,' 'No.'"
Matthew 5:34, 37a NKJV

THE STORY BEHIND WHAT JESUS SAID

On a hillside overlooking the Sea of Galilee, crowds gathered for several days to listen to Jesus teach. During that time, Jesus taught lots of different lessons. One was on the importance of being true to one's word.

The Jewish people knew that God's law, in the book of Leviticus, said, "Do not lie under oath." So they believed that if they didn't make an oath—swearing to do something by adding God's name or something related to him after their promise—they were free to lie. Jesus challenged them to simply speak the truth. If they said they were going to do something, they should just do it, regardless of whether they made an oath or not.

20   J E S U S   S P E A K S

It was almost time for the toughest final. The teacher had announced a month ahead of time that it would be open book, but only a week before the exam she changed her mind. No texts would be allowed. The class erupted with complaints. The teacher had made a promise, but her word wasn't good.

The disciples knew Jesus was as good as his word. He would never break a promise. His *yes* never meant "unless I change my mind" or "until something better comes along." He was, and is, a friend whose word can be trusted.

That's the kind of friend, student, and son or daughter God wants you to be. He wants you to be someone who thinks carefully before making a commitment, someone who comes through even when it's inconvenient, someone whose word can be trusted to be the truth, the whole truth, and nothing but the truth—even without the "so help me God."

ONE FINAL THOUGHT

If your words can be trusted to be true, then your promises can be trusted to be kept, and you will be trusted by many.

TIMELESS WISDOM FOR EVERYDAY LIVING

True to Your Word

A promise is a promise. . . . God is present, watching and holding you to account.

Matthew 23:20 THE MESSAGE

Promises may get friends, but it is performance that must nurse and keep them.

Owen Felltham

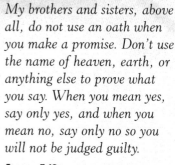

My brothers and sisters, above all, do not use an oath when you make a promise. Don't use the name of heaven, earth, or anything else to prove what you say. When you mean yes, say only yes, and when you mean no, say only no so you will not be judged guilty.

James 5:12 NCV

Keep your word even when it costs you.

Psalm 15:4b THE MESSAGE

My yes means yes because Jesus Christ, the Son of God, never wavers between yes and no. . . . For all of God's promises have been fulfilled in him.

2 Corinthians 1:18–20a NLT

Unfaithfulness in the keeping of an appointment is the act of dishonesty. You may as well borrow a person's money as his time. Horace Mann

He who is slow in promising is always the most faithful in performing.
Henri Rousseau

There is a living God. He has spoken in the Bible. He means what he says and will do all he has promised.
Hudson Taylor

It is better to say nothing than to promise something that you don't follow through on.
Ecclesiastes 5:5 NLT

Keep On Keeping On

Jesus said, "Keep on asking, and you will be given what you ask for. Keep on looking, and you will find. Keep on knocking, and the door will be opened. For everyone who asks, receives. Everyone who seeks, finds."
MATTHEW 7:7–8a NLT

THE STORY BEHIND WHAT JESUS SAID

Over the past several days, the crowds had heard Jesus say things that sounded next to impossible. "Love your enemies." "Don't worry about the food or drink you need to live." "Don't break your promises." Jesus knew that without God's help the words he was speaking would be nothing more than a self-help pep talk. If those who were listening tried to accomplish these goals on their own, their efforts would ultimately fail.

That's why Jesus told the crowds to keep asking, seeking, and knocking. God was listening. He had the power to help them do the impossible; all they had to do was continue to rely on him.

REFLECTIONS ON THE WORDS OF JESUS

If you want to master the bass line from your favorite song, you need to do more than buy a bass guitar. You need to learn how to play. Over time, with a few lessons and consistent practice, you'll be able to do what at first was impossible—play that bass line effortlessly.

Asking God to be a part of your life is like plugging your bass into an amp. It gives you the power you need to perform. The consistent practice of turning to God day after day will help you succeed when things get tough.

Jesus said to keep on asking (praying), seeking (looking for God at work in your life and the world), and knocking (relying on God's power to help you do what he asks). Keeping your life in tune with God in this way is the key to making a positive difference in the world around you.

ONE FINAL THOUGHT

Day by day, as you keep on seeking God, his power will work through your life to help turn the difficult into the doable.

TIMELESS WISDOM FOR EVERYDAY LIVING

Keep On Keeping On

Let us draw near to God with a sincere heart in full assurance of faith.

Hebrews 10:22a NIV

Let us leave the surface and, without leaving the world, plunge into God.

Teilhard de Chardin

When you search for me, you will find me; if you seek me with all your heart, I will let you find me, says the LORD.

Jeremiah 29:13–14a NRSV

Best of all is, God is with us.

John Wesley

I pray to you, O LORD; you hear my voice in the morning; at sunrise I offer my prayer and wait for your answer.

Psalm 5:2b–3 GNT

Seeking with faith, hope, and love pleases our Lord, and finding him pleases the soul, filling it full of joy. And so I learnt that as long as God allows us to struggle on this earth, seeking is as good as seeing.

Julian of Norwich

As the deer pants for streams of water, so I long for you, O God. I thirst for God, the living God. When can I come and stand before him?

Psalm 42:1–2 NLT

God . . . isn't far from any of us, and he gives us the power to live, to move, and to be who we are.

Acts 17:27–28a CEV

I have so much business I cannot get on without spending three hours daily in prayer.

Martin Luther

Trouble Happens

Jesus said, "In this world you will have trouble, but be brave! I have defeated the world."

JOHN 16:33b NCV

THE STORY BEHIND WHAT JESUS SAID

In a few hours, Jesus would appear totally defeated. His closest friends would abandon him. He would refuse to defend himself when on trial. While nailed to a cross, Jesus would cry out to his Father, asking why he'd been left alone.

Knowing all this lay ahead, Jesus still told his disciples he had "defeated the world." He spoke in the past tense, like he'd already battled death and won. Jesus wasn't just trying to keep a positive attitude. He was telling his disciples what he knew was true. Trouble was ahead for him, just like it was ahead for the disciples. But that wasn't cause for fear. It was time for courage. Victory was certain.

REFLECTIONS ON THE WORDS OF JESUS

It's another Friday night at the movies and it looks like the hero is really in trouble this time. His snowboard getaway has failed. His martial arts skills have come up short. The bad guys have samurai swords and hot tempers. Then the guy next to you says, "Relax, I saw this movie last week. The ninja girlfriend shows up and saves him."

Once you know the ending, even a nail-biter of a story doesn't seem as frightening. The same is true with the story of your life. Some chapters may leave you feeling defeated or afraid, but you know the end of the story, just like Jesus did.

God has promised to work out every detail of your life, even in situations that seem hopeless, in a way that will end up bringing good things your way. Hold on to hope when trouble comes. Something good is just around the corner. A happy ending is on its way.

ONE FINAL THOUGHT

No trouble will ever come your way that God doesn't have the power, desire, and plan to use in a positive way in your life.

TIMELESS WISDOM
FOR EVERYDAY LIVING

Trouble Happens

God is our shelter and strength, always ready to help in times of trouble. Psalm 46:1 GNT

We know that in everything God works for the good of those who love him.

Romans 8:28a NCV

Have courage for the great sorrows of life, and patience for the small ones. And when you have laboriously accomplished your daily task, go to sleep in peace. God is awake.

Victor Hugo

Sunshine without rain is the recipe for a desert. Arab Proverb

Troubles are often the tools by which God fashions us for better things.

Henry Ward Beeche

These troubles and sufferings of ours are, after all, quite small and won't last very long. Yet this short time of distress will result in God's richest blessing upon us forever and ever!

2 Corinthians 4:17 TLB

It has done me good to be somewhat parched by the heat and drenched by the rain of life.

Henry Wadsworth Longfellow

I am sure that God, who began the good work within you, will continue his work until it is finally finished on that day when Christ Jesus comes back again.

Philippians 1:6 NLT

Whenever trouble comes your way, let it be an opportunity for joy.

James 1:2 NLT

Be Original—Be Yourself

Jesus said, "All this time and money wasted on fashion—do you think it makes that much difference? Instead of looking at the fashions, walk out into the fields and look at the wildflowers."
MATTHEW 6:28 THE MESSAGE

THE STORY BEHIND WHAT JESUS SAID

The crowd outside Capernaum had been listening to Jesus for quite a while. Though they were intent on hearing every word, at times their minds may have begun to wander. Looking from Jesus to those around them, they may have been distracted by their own personal anxieties and problems.

Jesus knew all about their everyday worries and concerns, and he redirected the crowd's focus to a God-given visual aid. He pointed out the wildflowers. They didn't stress out or worry. They didn't give in to distress or agitation. They simply bloomed the way God had created them, each one unique and beautiful.

REFLECTIONS ON THE WORDS OF JESUS

A field of purple wildflowers may look like each flower is just like all the rest when seen from a distance. A closer look, however, reveals subtle differences in their height, the number of leaves—even the hue of their petals. That doesn't make one any better than another. It just makes it different.

You are much more intricate than a flower. You're also much more precious. God took great care in designing you as a one-of-a-kind creation, never to be duplicated since the dawn of time. Your beauty comes from deep inside, beyond that first layer of skin.

God's will for you is for you simply to be you, to delight in God's glorious creation. You have a special place in this world. Only you can fill it perfectly.

ONE FINAL THOUGHT

Seeing yourself through God's eyes means delighting in being the unique individual he designed.

TIMELESS WISDOM FOR EVERYDAY LIVING

Be Original—Be Yourself

How you made me is amazing and wonderful. I praise you for that. Psalm 139:14a NIRV

God's fingers can touch nothing but to mold it into loveliness.

George MacDonald

Don't be concerned about the outward beauty that depends on jewelry, or beautiful clothes, or hair arrangement. Be beautiful inside, in your hearts, with the lasting charm of a gentle and quiet spirit which is so precious to God.

1 Peter 3:3—4 TLB

God does not judge by outward appearances.

Galatians 2:6 GNT

Beauty is God's handwriting. Welcome it in every fair face, every fair day, every fair flower. Charles Kingsley

You never know yourself until you know more than your body. The image of God is not sealed in the features of your face, but in the lineaments of your soul. Thomas Traherne

God passes through the thicket of the world, and wherever his glance falls he turns all things to beauty.

Saint John of the Cross

When you look into water, you see a likeness of your face. When you look into your heart, you see what you are really like.

Proverbs 27:19 NIRV

God writes the gospel not in the Bible alone, but on trees, and flowers, and clouds, and stars.

Martin Luther

The Cycle of Thanks

Jesus said, "Weren't ten men healed? Where are the other nine? Is this Samaritan the only one who came back to thank God?" Then Jesus said to him, "Stand up and go on your way. You were healed because you believed."
LUKE 17:17–19 NCV

THE STORY BEHIND WHAT JESUS SAID

Ten lepers stood outside the village, outcasts because of their disfiguring disease. Keeping their distance, as law required, they called out to Jesus. They'd been shunned and rejected before. They dared not ask for healing. All they begged for was mercy. Jesus gladly gave them both. He then told them to show themselves to the priests, who would declare their once contagious bodies clean and healthy again.

The men left at once. Along the way, their leprous sores disappeared. Though ten had been healed, only one returned—a Samaritan, who even when healed would still be considered an outcast among the Jews. But gratitude drew him back to Jesus, the one who fully accepted him, sick or healthy, Samaritan or Jew.

Gratitude isn't mandatory. Just as the lepers didn't have to thank Jesus for what he did for them, you're not required to thank God for all he has given you. However, just because gratitude isn't mandatory doesn't mean it's unimportant.

Being grateful is a loving way of living life. It begins by recognizing when God and others do things for you just because they love you. Showing your appreciation is a way of returning that love.

The more often you take time to say thank-you to God, the more you'll notice how much you have to be thankful for. The more thankful you feel, the more satisfied you'll be with what you have. The more satisfied you are, the happier you'll be—and the more grateful you'll feel toward God. It's a cycle that honors God while helping you really enjoy life.

ONE FINAL THOUGHT

God encourages you to be grateful not for his own benefit so much as for the happiness of your own heart.

TIMELESS WISDOM FOR EVERYDAY LIVING

The Cycle of Thanks

Thou hast given so much to me. Give me one more thing—a grateful heart.

George Herbert

Whatever happens, keep thanking God because of Jesus Christ. This is what God wants you to do.

1 Thessalonians 5:18 CEV

In ordinary life we hardly realize that we receive a great deal more than we give, and that it is only with gratitude that life becomes rich.

Dietrich Bonhoeffer

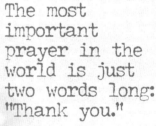

The most important prayer in the world is just two words long: "Thank you."

Meister Eckhart

Always use the name of our Lord Jesus Christ to thank God the Father for everything.

Ephesians 5:20 CEV

We give thanks to you, O God, we give thanks to you! We proclaim how great you are and tell of the wonderful things you have done. Psalm 75:1 GNT

My God will use his wonderful riches in Christ Jesus to give you everything you need.
Philippians 4:19 NCV

Let us be grateful to people who make us happy—they are the charming gardens who make our souls blossom.
Marcel Proust

Were there no God in this glorious world with grateful hearts: and no one to thank.
Christina Rosetti

Believe It or Not

Jesus said, "God loved the world so much that he gave his only Son, so that everyone who believes in him may not die but have eternal life."
JOHN 3:16 GNT

THE STORY BEHIND WHAT JESUS SAID

Nicodemus watched the sun set. He knew what the other religious leaders called Jesus—a lunatic, a liar. But there was something about this Teacher that intrigued him, something even a Pharisee like himself couldn't explain away.

Under the cover of darkness, Nicodemus brought his questions to Jesus. Jesus' answers were unlike anything Nicodemus had heard before. Nicodemus learned he had to be born a second time, spiritually instead of physically. Then Jesus spoke of God's incredible love. Jesus said all Nicodemus had to do was believe his words—nothing more, nothing less—and Nicodemus would live forever. In Nicodemus's heart, he knew his search for the truth was over. The only thing left to do was believe.

REFLECTIONS ON THE WORDS OF JESUS

Some offers sound too good to be true. "Free car with every tank of gas!" "Lose ten pounds in ten days on the all-you-can-eat chili-cheese-fries diet!" "Never study again by listening to tapes while you sleep!" When you see an offer like this, your mind immediately asks, "What's the catch?"

Jesus' offer of eternal life sounds too good to be true. All you have to do is believe that Jesus is who he said he is, and you receive a life that never ends. Talk about freebies! So what's the catch?

The catch is that this gift is anything but free. It came at the cost of Jesus' life. Jesus, being obedient to the Father, paid the ultimate price for you to spend eternity with him. That's how deep his love for you goes. Just like Nicodemus, your heart is searching for the truth. The choice to believe it and act on it, once you've heard it, is up to you.

ONE FINAL THOUGHT

The only thing you can do to receive God's gift of life without end is to believe that what Jesus said is true.

TIMELESS WISDOM FOR EVERYDAY LIVING

Believe It or Not

God treats everyone alike. He accepts people only because they have faith in Jesus Christ.
Romans 3:22 CEV

God does not justify us because we are worthy, but by justifying us makes us worthy.

Thomas Watson

It is by grace you have been saved, through faith—and this not from yourselves, it is the gift of God—not by works, so that no one can boast. Ephesians 2:8–9 NIV

Christ has transformed all our sunsets into dawn.

Clement of Alexandria

Only Jesus has the power to save! His name is the only one in all the world that can save anyone.

Acts 4:12 CEV

God wants everyone to be saved and to know the whole truth, which is, There is only one God, and Christ Jesus is the only one who can bring us to God. 1 Timothy 2:4–5a CEV

We are never nearer Christ than when we find ourselves lost in a holy amazement at His unspeakable love. John Owen

Not only do we not know God except through Jesus Christ; we do not even know ourselves except through Jesus Christ.
Blaise Pascal

Christ made love the stairway that would enable all Christians to climb up to heaven. Fulgentius of Ruspe

43

Doing What Matters

Jesus said, "Love the Lord God with all your passion and prayer and intelligence and energy . . . [and] love others as well as yourself."
MARK 12:30–31 CEV

THE STORY BEHIND WHAT JESUS SAID

The religious leaders fired question after question at Jesus, but they weren't there to learn. They wanted to trick Jesus into saying something that would turn the crowds against him. However, one teacher of Jewish law wanted more from Jesus. He wanted real answers.

This teacher knew the religious laws—all 613 of them. He also knew how hard it was to keep them all. He asked Jesus which law was the most important, which law he should never fail to keep. Jesus knew the humble heart behind this question. He explained that loving God and loving others fulfilled every law. The other religious leaders fell silent as Jesus praised this one teacher's honest search for the truth.

JESUS SPEAKS

REFLECTIONS ON THE WORDS OF JESUS

When you're psyching yourself up to play a team sport, there's something you need to know: the rules. What counts and what doesn't. What helps your team and what hurts it. You need to know what it takes to win.

Life is not a game. Nevertheless, there are still rules that can help you live like a winner. The one rule that really matters is to love God and love those around you. In the end, it isn't really the actions you take but the motivations behind them that count.

When you're faced with a decision, you have the ball in your hands. You just need to decide what to do with it. Think about God. What's the best way to love him in this situation? Think about those people whom your decision will affect. What do you think Jesus would do if he were living your life? Once you make your decision, all that's left to do is play ball.

ONE FINAL THOUGHT

When it comes to making choices, loving God and others is always the right choice, no matter what the circumstance.

TIMELESS WISDOM FOR EVERYDAY LIVING

Doing What Matters

Love him totally who gave himself totally for your love. Claire of Assisi

We were born to love, we live to love, and we will die to love still more.

Joseph Cafasso

Love is kind and patient, never jealous, boastful, proud, or rude. Love isn't selfish or quick tempered. It doesn't keep a record of wrongs that others do. Love rejoices in the truth, but not in evil. Love is always supportive, loyal, hopeful, and trusting. Love never fails!

1 Corinthians 13:4–8a CEV

Let all that you do be done in love.

1 Corinthians 16:14 NASB

God is love. Those who live in love live in God, and God lives in them. 1 John 4:16b NCV

This is the miracle that happens every time to those who really love; the more they give, the more they possess. Ranier Maria Rilke

The more we love, the better we are, and the greater our friendships are, the dearer we are to God.

Jeremy Taylor

Our Lord does not care so much for the importance of our works as for the love with which they are done.

Saint Theresa of Avila

No one who loves others will harm them. So love is all that the Law demands. Romans 13:10 CEV

Prove It

Jesus said to Thomas,
"Put your finger here;
see my hands. Reach out
your hand and put it
into my side. Stop
doubting and believe."
JOHN 20:27 NIV

THE STORY BEHIND WHAT JESUS SAID

Thomas could hardly breathe. He glanced back at the door. The latch was still locked. Yet suddenly Jesus was standing before him. Alive! A hush fell over the disciples as Jesus' gaze rested on Thomas. They'd told Thomas they'd seen Jesus alive, but Thomas said he refused to believe their eyewitness account unless he could touch Jesus' wounds with his own hands.

Thomas felt the blood rushing to his cheeks. How could he have doubted the one who always did the impossible? Yet a single glance into Jesus' eyes reassured Thomas that the impossible had happened once more. Jesus didn't condemn Thomas for doubting. Jesus simply reached out in love, as he had to Thomas so many times before.

REFLECTIONS ON THE WORDS OF JESUS

When a physics class studies gravity, the teacher usually assigns experiments to prove that what's being taught is true. That's because both teachers and students know it's tough to believe what you cannot see.

God knows that's true as well. That's one reason why he encourages you to test and see that he's as real and as reliable as gravity. You can do this by taking your doubts and turning them into honest questions. Then look for answers by searching the Bible, talking to people who've known God longer than you have, and praying for God's wisdom to help you "stop doubting and believe."

But, just like science, sometimes you won't be able to understand it all. At times like that, your only answer will be found in trusting the words of the one who is eternally trustworthy. That's when you need to make a conscious choice to leave doubt behind, trust what you cannot see, and move ahead in faith.

ONE FINAL THOUGHT

Turn doubts into questions for God—ask him to give you the wisdom to understand what you can and the faith to trust him for what you can't.

TIMELESS WISDOM FOR EVERYDAY LIVING

Prove It

Faith makes us sure of what we hope for and gives us proof of what we cannot see.

Hebrews 11:1 CEV

Faith is believing what one cannot see, and the reward of faith is to see what one believes.

Saint Augustine of Hippo

In faith there is enough light for those who want to believe and enough shadows to blind those who don't.

Blaise Pascal

When the Son of Man returns, you will know it beyond all doubt.

Luke 17:24a NLT

All I have seen teaches me to trust the Creator for all I have not seen.

Ralph Waldo Emerson

Trust in the LORD with all your heart and lean not on your own understanding; in all your ways acknowledge him, and he will make your paths straight. Proverbs 3:5–6 NIV

Just as I am, though tossed about with many a conflict, many a doubt, fightings within, and fears without, O Lamb of God, I come.
Charlotte Elliott

If any of you need wisdom, you should ask God, and it will be given to you. God is generous and won't correct you for asking.
James 1:5 CEV

Believe God's word and power more than you believe your own feelings and experiences. Samuel Rutherford

It's Okay to Lose It

Jesus saw her weeping, and he saw how the people with her were weeping also; his heart was touched, and he was deeply moved. "Where have you buried him?" he asked them.
JOHN 11:33 GNT

THE STORY BEHIND WHAT JESUS SAID

Mary fell at Jesus' feet, heartbroken, her face wet with tears. She was glad Jesus had arrived to mourn the death of her brother, but why hadn't he come sooner? Jesus could have healed Lazarus. He could have taken away the reason for her tears.

Looking down at Mary, Jesus' own heart broke. Jesus knew God's power could bring Lazarus back to life. That didn't take away the pain he felt watching the sorrow of those around Him. Jesus' own eyes, the eyes of God, welled with tears. Watching Jesus weep, the other mourners could never have guessed that within moments, the only tears left would be those of joy as Jesus raised his friend from the dead.

REFLECTIONS ON THE WORDS OF JESUS

There is no right or wrong reason to cry. The heart of every individual, guy or girl, is wired a bit differently. While one person may cry buckets every time a certain song comes on the radio, another may not shed a single tear at a friend's funeral. No matter how frequently or infrequently you show your emotions to others, God asks that you share your deepest feelings with him.

Jesus knows what pain feels like. He faced the emotional pain of being betrayed by a friend and the physical pain of being beaten and crucified. Whatever you're feeling right now, he's been there. He doesn't just ache for you, he aches with you and wants to help dry your tears from the inside out.

When your heart's on overload, turn to God. Ask him to help you understand what's behind your emotions, face your pain head-on, and then express your feelings in an honest, helpful way.

ONE FINAL THOUGHT

Handling your emotions doesn't mean hiding them, but honestly sharing your deepest hurts with a God who knows exactly how you feel.

TIMELESS WISDOM FOR EVERYDAY LIVING

It's Okay to Lose It

We have a high priest who can feel it when we are weak and hurting. Hebrews 4:15a NIRV

The tearful praying Christian, whose distress prevents his words, will be clearly understood by the Most High.

Charles Haddon Spurgeon

The righteous cry out, and the LORD hears them; he delivers them from all their troubles. The LORD is close to the brokenhearted and saves those who are crushed in spirit.

Psalm 34:17–18 NIV

The glory of God is a person fully alive. Irenaeus

You keep track of all my sorrows. You have collected all my tears in your bottle. You have recorded each one in your book.

Psalm 56:8 NLT

Heaven knows we need never be ashamed of our tears, for they are rain upon the blinding dust of earth, overlying our hard hearts. Charles Dickens

Sorrow is a fruit; God does not allow it to grow on a branch that is too weak to bear it.

Victor Hugo

In sorrow and suffering, go straight to God with confidence, and you will be strengthened, enlightened, and instructed.

Saint John of the Cross

He heals those who have broken hearts. He takes care of their wounds. Psalm 147:3 NIRV

Always by Your Side

Jesus said, "I won't leave you like orphans. I will come back to you. In a little while the people of this world won't be able to see me, but you will see me. And because I live, you will live."
JOHN 14:18-19 CEV

THE STORY BEHIND WHAT JESUS SAID

What began as a celebration was now filled with tension and confusion. Judas had just hurried out of the room to betray Jesus. The disciples heard Jesus say he was going away to die. Fear and uncertainty replaced the quiet reverence of the evening's Passover celebration.

Having spent the last three years together, the disciples could not picture life without Jesus in it. What would they do? Where would they go? Would their lives be in danger, just like his? Jesus reassured his good friends with a promise. Not only would they see him again, but God's Spirit would actually live inside them. They would never face a day alone again, in this life or the next.

REFLECTIONS ON THE WORDS OF JESUS

When a close friend moves away, a relationship often changes. Though postcards, e-mails, and phone calls can help you keep in touch, nothing can ever take the place of spending one-on-one time with each other.

Having a relationship with God can feel like one of those long-distance relationships at times. Some days it may even seem like God is refusing to answer the phone. But what you feel doesn't always match up with what is true. The truth is that you're never alone. God is not just thinking about you, his Spirit is living inside you.

So the next time you feel alone, don't let your feelings convince you that you are. Call out to God. Tell him that you need to know he's near. Reread parts of the Bible, God's message to you, focusing on what Jesus did when he felt alone. Be still and listen. God is by your side, whispering words of love in unexpected ways.

ONE FINAL THOUGHT

With God in your life, there is no sorrow, no challenge, no misunderstanding, and no fear that you'll ever have to face alone.

TIMELESS WISDOM
FOR EVERYDAY LIVING

Always by Your Side

The Lord is near to all who call on him, to all who call on him in truth. Psalm 145:18 NIV

When Jesus is present, all is well, and nothing seems difficult.

Thomas à Kempis

We are pressed on every side by troubles, but we are not crushed and broken. We are perplexed, but we don't give up and quit. We are hunted down, but God never abandons us.

2 Corinthians 4:8–9 NLT

If God is with us, no one can defeat us.

Romans 8:31b NCV

What our Lord did was done with this intent, and this alone, that he might be with us and we with him.

Meister Eckhart

58

Since God assured us, "I'll never let you down, never walk off and leave you," we can boldly quote, "God is there, ready to help; I'm fearless no matter what. Who or what can get to me?" Hebrews 13:5–6 THE MESSAGE

It is when God appears to have abandoned us that we must abandon ourselves most wholly to God.

François Fénelon

The LORD your God is with you; his power gives you victory. The LORD will take delight in you, and in his love he will give you new life.

Zephaniah 3:17a GNT

God is always near you and with you; leave Him not alone.

Brother Lawrence

Cleaning Your Cranium

Jesus said, "What people say with their mouths comes from the way they think; these are the things that make people unclean."
MATTHEW 15:18 NCV

THE STORY BEHIND WHAT JESUS SAID

Jesus was ignoring important traditions of the Jewish faith, like washing his hands the right way or only eating foods Jewish law declared clean. The top Jewish leaders traveled close to a hundred miles to track down this hypocrite.

When they met, Jesus accused the leaders themselves of being hypocritical. He told the crowds that evil thoughts and actions, not what they ate, made them clean or unclean. Noticing the Pharisees were offended, the disciples nervously cautioned Jesus. But Jesus wouldn't take back what he said. His job was to tell the truth, regardless of whether it was popular or not.

You have a cold that just won't quit. You're coughing. You're sneezing. Your head feels like it's filled with last week's dirty gym socks. You're under attack from germs you can't even see. Symptoms like these are usually your first clue that an "unclean" germ has invaded your body.

The same can be true of your mind. Unkind words and actions are visible symptoms of a mind that has let in thoughts that don't belong there. The best prevention for this kind of mental attack is filling your mind with things that would make God smile—thoughts that are true, good, and loving. One way to do that is to choose with care what movies, magazines, music, and conversations you allow your mind to dwell on.

When an unclean thought pops into your mind, deal with it before the infection can spread. Take it to God. Ask him to help you erase it and then replace it with the truth.

ONE FINAL THOUGHT

What you choose to think about will affect both your speech and actions, so choose wisely—fill your mind with things God would approve of.

TIMELESS WISDOM FOR EVERYDAY LIVING

Cleaning Your Cranium

Nurture your mind with great thoughts; to believe in the heroic makes heroes. Benjamin Disraeli

Every thought is a seed. If you plant crab apples, don't count on harvesting Golden Delicious.

Author Unknown

Fix your thoughts on what is true and honorable and right. Think about things that are pure and lovely and admirable. Think about things that are excellent and worthy of praise.

Philippians 4:8 NLT

You will keep in perfect peace all who trust in you.

Isaiah 26:3a NLT

Occupy your mind with good thoughts, or the enemy will fill it with bad ones: unoccupied it cannot be.

Sir Thomas More

The word of God is full of living power. It is sharper than the sharpest knife, cutting deep into our innermost thoughts and desires. It exposes us for what we really are. Hebrews 4:12 NLT

It is not enough to have a good mind. The main thing is to use it well.

René Descartes

We destroy people's arguments and every proud thing that raises itself against the knowledge of God. We capture every thought and make it give up and obey Christ.

2 Corinthians 10:4b–5 NCV

Live under the control of the Holy Spirit. If you do, you will think about what the Spirit wants. Romans 8:5b NIRV

Undeserved Freedom

They nailed Jesus to a cross. They also nailed the two criminals to crosses, one on each side of Jesus. Jesus said, "Father, forgive these people! They don't know what they're doing."
LUKE 23:33b–34 CEV

THE STORY BEHIND WHAT JESUS SAID

The hill outside of Jerusalem was in emotional chaos. The cheers of victory and sounds of mocking laughter threatened to drown out the quiet sobs of grief from the group of women who had gathered below Christ's cross. Through a haze of pain, Jesus looked out over them all . . . the women who believed in him, the men who'd nailed him to the cross, the soldiers making fun of him while preparing to gamble for his clothing, the two guilty criminals who shared his death sentence.

Jesus looked up, asking his Father for one thing—not for himself, but for those below, as well as for every other person whose sins had nailed him to that cross. He asked for forgiveness.

REFLECTIONS ON THE WORDS OF JESUS

Everyone blows it. That includes your friends, your folks, and you. God doesn't ask you to keep score or ignore the wrongs that have been done. What he asks is that you follow his example and forgive.

There's freedom in forgiveness. It's more than just a second chance. It's a fresh start. It's like getting a D on a test but having your teacher drop your lowest score before averaging your final grade. It's like that D never happened. Because of what Jesus did on the cross, the wrong choices you've made have been erased. They no longer count against you.

Accepting God's forgiveness changes your relationship with him in the same way that being forgiven by a friend allows you to freely enjoy each other's company again. You don't have to be embarrassed over the past, worry about payback time, or be afraid of what God thinks about you. You're fully forgiven and unconditionally loved.

ONE FINAL THOUGHT

Because God has fully forgiven you, you can enjoy a loving relationship with him that's free of fear, guilt, and shame.

TIMELESS WISDOM FOR EVERYDAY LIVING

Undeserved Freedom

He who cannot forgive breaks the bridge over which he himself must pass. George Herbert

Forgiveness is the answer to the child's dream of a miracle by which what is broken is made whole again, what is soiled is again made clean.

Dag Hammarskjöld

[God] has removed our sins as far away from us as the east is from the west.
Psalm 103:12 TLB

If we confess our sins to God, he can always be trusted to forgive us.
1 John 1:9 CEV

If you kept a record of our sins, who could escape being condemned? But you forgive us, so that we should stand in awe of you. Psalm 130:3–4 GNT

Always do these things: Show mercy to others, be kind, humble, gentle, and patient. Get along with each other, and forgive each other. If someone does wrong to you, forgive that person because the Lord forgave you. Colossians 3:12b–13 NCV

You are a forgiving God, gracious and compassionate, slow to anger and abounding in love.

Nehemiah 9:17b NIV

Who takes vengeance or bears a grudge acts like one who, having cut one hand while handling a knife, avenges himself by stabbing the other hand.

The Jerusalem Talmud

Forgiveness is not an occasional art, it is a permanent attitude.

Martin Luther

You Can Count on Me

Jesus said, "The
dependable manager . . .
is a blessed man if
when the master shows
up he's doing his job.
Luke 12:42b–43
THE MESSAGE

THE STORY BEHIND WHAT JESUS SAID

Jesus left the crowds behind, turning his full attention to his small, handpicked group of disciples. He wanted to prepare them for his death as well as for his future return. So Jesus told them a story about those who chose to continue his work on earth.

Jesus spoke of a master who took a trip and left his house in the care of trusted servants. As the master's absence grew longer, some of the servants began to slack off in their work. After all, there was no master to check up on them. When the master surprised them one day with his sudden return, he rewarded the responsible servants, as well as the lazy ones, according to what they'd done.

REFLECTIONS ON THE WORDS OF JESUS

Throughout history, God has chosen teens just like you to do amazing things. Josiah ruled a kingdom throughout his teen years, having become king at the age of eight. David was about fifteen when he knocked off a giant. Mary probably gave birth to Jesus in her mid-teens. Who knows what God has planned for you?

The teenage years are not a holding pattern to keep you busy until you're old enough to do what really matters. If you're ready to put your whole heart into whatever God brings your way, God can use you right now to do incredible things.

Some of those tasks may not seem all that incredible to you—folding your laundry, doing your homework, or playing checkers with your little brother, for instance. But you never know what God is going to do with your efforts. The more faithful you are in the little things today, the bigger the responsibilities God knows he can trust you with tomorrow.

ONE FINAL THOUGHT

When you strive for excellence in everything you do, God knows he can entrust you with even greater responsibility.

TIMELESS WISDOM FOR EVERYDAY LIVING

You Can Count on Me

Through the Word we are put together and shaped up for the tasks God has for us.

2 Timothy 3:17 THE MESSAGE

Work hard and cheerfully at whatever you do, as though you were working for the Lord rather than for people. Colossians 3:23 NLT

Great works do not always lie in our way, but every moment we may do little ones excellently, that is, with great love.

Saint Francis de Sales

No matter what you do, work at it with all your might.

Ecclesiastes 9:10a NIRV

The smallest things become great when God requires them of us; they are small only in themselves; they are always great when they are done for God.

François Fénelon

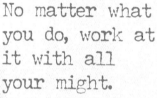

God can do anything, you know—far more than you could ever imagine or guess or request in your wildest dreams! He does it not by pushing us around but by working within us, his Spirit deeply and gently within us.

Ephesians 3:20 THE MESSAGE

Action springs not from thought, but from a readiness for responsibility.

Deitrich Bonhoeffer

Few things help an individual more than to place responsibility upon him and to let him know that you trust him.

Booker T. Washington

There are three stages in the work of God: Impossible; Difficult; Done.

Hudson Taylor

Love at Work

> The ones who pleased the Lord will ask, "When did we give you something to eat or drink? . . . The king will answer, "Whenever you did it for any of my people, no matter how unimportant they seemed, you did it for me."
> MATTHEW 25:37–40 CEV

THE STORY BEHIND WHAT JESUS SAID

Five hundred years before Jesus was born, the prophet Zechariah predicted the future Messiah would stand on the Mount of Olives to establish his rule over the earth. This exact spot, overlooking the Temple, was where Jesus held a private discussion with his disciples. They asked him about the future, when the end of the world would take place.

Jesus responded with several parables. He emphasized that focusing on doing the right thing right now had an impact on the future. Those whose loving actions proved they truly believed what Jesus said would be honored by Jesus' Father, the king. Knowing "when" the end would come wasn't as important as sharing God's love with others where they were right now.

JESUS SPEAKS

REFLECTIONS ON THE WORDS OF JESUS

When God created the world, he didn't ensure that every person had the same advantages as everyone else. Consequently, there are rich people, poor people, and everyone in between. Just looking at the lives of kids in your very own school, you can see that not everyone's finances, health, or opportunities are even.

God chose to make people dependent on one another, which teaches them how to put love into action. Love doesn't stand around and watch someone suffer when it has the ability to help. Love reaches out—even when it's inconvenient or uncomfortable. Love means sharing something that's valuable to you.

You don't have to have money to love those in need. Be generous with your time and talents. Volunteer at a soup kitchen. Tutor at school. Be a friend to someone who's hurting. Reach out right now with what you have where you are. What you give to others you give to God.

ONE FINAL THOUGHT

One way of loving God is to help meet the needs of others by sacrificially giving your own valuable time, talents, and resources.

TIMELESS WISDOM FOR EVERYDAY LIVING

Love at Work

Give what you have. To someone else it may be better than you dare to think.

Henry Wadsworth Longfellow

If you oppress poor people, you insult the God who made them; but kindness shown to the poor is an act of worship.

Proverbs 14:31 GNT

Command the rich to do what is good. Tell them to be rich in doing good things. They must give freely. They must be willing to share. In that way they will put riches away for themselves.

1 Timothy 6:18–19a NIRV

Share with God's people who need help.

Romans 12:13a NCV

Not what you possess but what you do with what you have determines your true worth.

Thomas Carlyle

JESUS SPEAKS

Happy are those who are concerned for the poor; the LORD will help them when they are in trouble. The LORD will protect them and preserve their lives; he will make them happy in the land. Psalm 41:1-2a GNT

If you help the poor, you are lending to the LORD—and he will repay you! Proverbs 19:17 NLT

Remember that when you leave this earth, you can take with you nothing you have received—only what you have given: a full heart enriched by honest service, love, sacrifice, and courage.

Saint Francis of Assisi

You can give without loving, but you cannot love without giving.

Amy Carmichael

Reaching the Critical Point

Jesus said, "Be easy
on people; you'll find
life a lot easier.
Give away your life;
you'll find life
given back."
LUKE 6:37b–38a
THE MESSAGE

THE STORY BEHIND WHAT JESUS SAID

Jesus' ministry was just beginning, but already the religious leaders were jealous of his popularity. They looked for ways to discredit him in front of his followers, criticizing Jesus' actions without considering the motivations behind them. However, the Pharisees' words didn't influence the large number of disciples, or "learners," following Jesus.

Soon after being ridiculed by the Pharisees, Jesus went to the top of a mountain and prayed all night. The next morning Jesus chose twelve apostles, or messengers, from the crowd of disciples. To prepare these messengers to share God's message of love, Jesus spoke to them about the power of their words. Jesus wanted the words they said, unlike the words of the Pharisees, to build others up instead of tear them down.

JESUS SPEAKS

Critics can be helpful. Hearing that a movie received "two thumbs down" can help you decide whether or not to buy a ticket. Critics who review the arts usually have one thing in common—expertise. They are paid to know what they're talking about.

When it comes to being critical of people, the true expert is God. No one else knows the whole story behind a person's actions. That's why God is the only one able to judge someone's life. When people give in to the urge to put others down, what they're really doing is playing God.

Before critical words make it across your lips, take your eyes off the object of your criticism and take an honest look at yourself. Ask yourself if you're being critical because your feelings have been hurt. Question whether jealousy or pride plays a part in your judgment. Ask God to help you deal with what's behind your criticism before it spills over onto someone else.

ONE FINAL THOUGHT

Only God is qualified to judge people's lives, so ask him to turn your critical thoughts into a time of reflection about what's really going on inside you.

TIMELESS WISDOM FOR EVERYDAY LIVING

Reaching the Critical Point

Treat your friends as you do your pictures, and place them in their best light.

Jennie Jerome Churchill

Words kill, words give life; they're either poison or fruit—you choose.

Proverbs 18:21 THE MESSAGE

Don't speak evil against each other, my dear brothers and sisters. If you criticize each other and condemn each other, then you are criticizing and condemning God's law.

James 4:11a NLT

How much easier it is to be critical than to be correct.

Benjamin Disraeli

Some people like to make cutting remarks, but the words of the wise soothe and heal.

Proverbs 12:18 TLB

The whole Law can be summed up in this one command: "Love others as you love yourself." But if instead of showing love among yourselves you are always critical and catty, watch out! Beware of ruining each other.

Galatians 5:14–15 TLB

If we had no faults, we should take less pleasure in noticing those of others.

François de La Rochefoucauld

If you want to find rest here below, and hereafter, in all circumstances say, Who am I? and do not judge anybody.

Joseph of Panephysis

How rarely we weigh our neighbor in the same balance in which we weigh ourselves. Thomas à Kempis

Everybody Has a Story

When Jesus was getting into the boat, the man begged to go with him. But Jesus would not let him. Instead, he said, "Go home to your family and tell them how much the Lord has done for you and how good he has been to you."

MARK 5:18–19 CEV

THE STORY BEHIND WHAT JESUS SAID

The limestone caves were more than a cemetery for the dead. They were home for a wild man. His violent screams resounded through the village as he beat himself with stones. People couldn't reason with him. Chains couldn't hold him. Yet a command from the Son of God freed him from the evil presence that tormented him.

Once God's power changed his life, the man longed to do what the disciples had done—drop everything and follow Jesus. On the other hand, the townspeople were terrified by Jesus' power and begged him to leave them alone. Knowing the man's personal experience could reach people who refused to listen to Jesus' own words, Jesus instructed the man to "follow" him by remaining right where he was.

REFLECTIONS ON THE WORDS OF JESUS

Suppose you found the cure for cancer. All you had to do was drink from a certain fountain and cancer cells would disappear. You wouldn't keep a discovery like that to yourself. You'd want the world to know that hope and healing was only a sip away.

Sharing what God has done in your life offers greater hope and healing than a cure for cancer. However, the fear of what others may think often holds people back. The truth is, you know something that can change someone's life—and eternal destiny.

Tell your story. Talk about how knowing God makes a difference in your life. You don't need a heart-stopping testimony or public speaking ability. Just be yourself. Answer questions honestly, even if the answer is "I don't know." Let the way you live tell the rest of the story. Ask God to use what you've shared. It's your job to tell your story. It's God's job to change hearts.

ONE FINAL THOUGHT

Letting God use your life to help others see him more clearly is as simple as telling your own story honestly and openly.

TIMELESS WISDOM FOR EVERYDAY LIVING

Everybody Has a Story

I try to find common ground with everyone so that I might bring them to Christ.

1 Corinthians 9:22b NLT

Preach not because you have to say something, but because you have something to say.

Richard Whately

You must worship Christ as Lord of your life. And if you are asked about your Christian hope, always be ready to explain it. But you must do this in a gentle and respectful way.

1 Peter 3:15–16a NLT

Preach the gospel at all times; if necessary, use words.

Saint Francis of Assisi

We know what it means to respect the Lord, and we encourage everyone to turn to him.

2 Corinthians 5:11a CEV

When you are with unbelievers, always make good use of the time. Be pleasant and hold their interest when you speak the message. Choose your words carefully and be ready to give answers to anyone who asks questions.

Colossians 4:5—6 CEV

When the people see that you truly love them, they will hear anything from you.

Richard Baxter

It is a great deal better to live a holy life than to talk about it. Lighthouses do not ring bells and fire cannons to call attention to their shining—they just shine.

Dwight L. Moody

What you are shouts so loud in my ears that I cannot hear what you say. Ralph Waldo Emerson

Real Life Riches

Jesus said, "Beware!
Don't be greedy for
what you don't have.
Real life is not
measured by how
much we own."
LUKE 12:15 NLT

THE STORY BEHIND WHAT JESUS SAID

The man pushed through the large crowd, unable to get close to Jesus. Discouraged, he simply shouted over the crowd, "Teacher, please tell my brother to divide our father's estate with me." Instead of trying to settle this disagreement between brothers, Jesus went straight to the heart of the matter—the man's own greedy heart.

Jesus told a story about a rich landowner who spent his whole life trying to become even wealthier. The landowner hoped one day he'd be rich enough to be able to sit back and enjoy life. However, the man's life ended that very night. Jesus told the brother that God declared the rich man a fool for wasting his life trying to gain what had no lasting value.

REFLECTIONS ON THE WORDS OF JESUS

Think of your most prized possession. It could be a basketball trophy, a necklace given to you by your best friend, a drum set you saved for months to buy, or even a stuffed animal you carted around everywhere when you were a kid. Now place your most prized possession next to the person you love most. Which do you treasure more?

The answer seems obvious. However, many people live their lives as though things matter more than people. They spend their time and energy doing whatever allows them to buy the best "stuff," and yet stuff doesn't last into eternity. Only God and people do.

You are at a point where you're getting ready to make big decisions about your future. What you treasure most highly in your heart will affect how you choose to live your life. To make your life really count means investing it in something that lasts.

ONE FINAL THOUGHT

Investing your life in what lasts is the key to gaining true treasure—riches that can only be stored in the heart.

TIMELESS WISDOM FOR EVERYDAY LIVING

Real Life Riches

Nothing that is God is obtainable by money.
Tertullian

It is certain that all that will go to heaven hereafter begin their heaven now, and have their hearts there.

Matthew Henry

Tell the rich people to do good, to be rich in doing good deeds, to be generous and ready to share. By doing that, they will be saving a treasure for themselves as a strong foundation for the future.

1 Timothy 6:18–19a NCV

It is by spending oneself that one becomes rich.

Sarah Bernhardt

The greatest good you can do for another is not just to share your riches but to reveal to him his own.

Benjamin Disraeli

Do not weary yourself to gain wealth, cease from your consideration of it. When you set your eyes on it, it is gone. For wealth certainly makes itself wings like an eagle that flies toward the heavens.
Proverbs 23:4–5 NASB

We are rich only through what we give; and poor only through what we refuse and keep.
Anne Swetchine

Whoever loves money never has money enough; whoever loves wealth is never satisfied with his income.
Ecclesiastes 5:10a NIV

Jesus said, "Wherever your treasure is, there your heart and thoughts will also be." Luke 12:34 NLT

Right on Time

Jesus said, "This sickness will not end in death. It is for the glory of God, to bring glory to the Son of God." Jesus loved Martha and her sister and Lazarus. But when he heard that Lazarus was sick, he stayed where he was for two more days.

JOHN 11:4–6 NCV

THE STORY BEHIND WHAT JESUS SAID

As Mary and Martha buried their brother, their grief was mixed with disbelief. *Where is Jesus when we need him most?* they must have thought. They knew people in Judea were searching for Jesus, not to listen to him speak, but to kill him. *Certainly fear wouldn't have kept Jesus from returning to heal a friend he loved so deeply?*

It wasn't fear, a lack of compassion, or a busy schedule that kept Jesus away. It was his perfect sense of timing. After three days in the hot Palestinian climate, a body would begin to decay. Waiting to arrive until then proved God could do the impossible. Jesus wouldn't settle for doing something good, when he could do something extraordinary.

REFLECTIONS ON THE WORDS OF JESUS

God's timing doesn't always feel as perfect as it is. That's because waiting feels more like being stuck in one place than moving forward. When you feel like God has hit the pause button on a situation in your life, don't give up hope. God's doing more than teaching you patience. God's hard at work to provide you with his very best.

God sees the big picture of your life, your plans, and your prayers. He knows what's ahead, both the potential obstacles and victories. He's willing to wait for the perfect time to act— the time that will help you and those around you experience his power and love most clearly.

When you find yourself waiting on God's perfect timing, keep on moving forward. Do what you need to do in other areas of your life. Keep praying, reminding yourself God's listening and working, even when you can't yet see the final, perfect results.

ONE FINAL THOUGHT

Waiting for God's perfect timing means waiting for God's best—so wait expectantly, knowing God is in the process of accomplishing something good in your life.

TIMELESS WISDOM FOR EVERYDAY LIVING

Right on Time

If we look forward to something we don't have yet, we must wait patiently and confidently.

Romans 8:25 NLT

There is no place for faith if we expect God to fulfill immediately what he promises.

John Calvin

God says, "At just the right time, I heard you. On the day of salvation, I helped you." Indeed, God is ready to help you right now.

2 Corinthians 6:2a NLT

Obedience is the fruit of faith; patience the bloom on the fruit.

Christina Rosetti

I was patient while I waited for the LORD. He turned to me and heard my cry for help.

Psalm 40:1 NIRV

The LORD is good to everyone who trusts in him, so it is best for us to wait in patience—to wait for him to save us—and it is best to learn this patience in our youth. Lamentations 3:25–27 GNT

We must wait for God, long, meekly, in the wind and wet, in the thunder and lightning, in the cold and in the dark. Wait, and he will come.

Frederick William Faber

Frequently the richest answers are not the speediest. . . . A prayer may be all the longer on its voyage because it is bringing us a heavier freight of blessing.

Charles Spurgeon

Quiet waiting before God would save [us] from many a mistake and from many a sorrow. Hudson Taylor

Refocusing on Reality

Jesus said, "Give your entire attention to what God is doing right now, and don't get worked up about what may or may not happen tomorrow. God will help you deal with whatever hard things come up when the time comes."
MATTHEW 6:34 THE MESSAGE

THE STORY BEHIND WHAT JESUS SAID

Jesus finished explaining to his disciples and a crowd of thousands that if they kept God and his work in the world as their top priority, God promised to take care of their needs. Jesus knew that simply saying these words wouldn't erase worry from people's minds, and so Jesus also spoke to their common sense.

When Jesus talked about hard times, he used an Aramaic word commonly used to describe the kind of damage hail-storms can do to crops. People recognize that this kind of trouble is out of their control; even today weather-related disasters are often called "acts of God." Jesus was remind-ing people not to worry about what they couldn't control, just to do what God asked.

REFLECTIONS ON THE WORDS OF JESUS

There are things that haven't happened yet that you need to be concerned about—giving an oral presentation in class tomorrow, making your allowance stretch another week, or comforting your friend who is having surgery in a couple of days. Being concerned about these things pushes you to take action. It can push you to study, to budget, or to pray for your friend.

Concern becomes worry when it fills your heart with fear instead of pushes you toward action. Worry can ruin your health, distract you from accomplishing what's important, and weaken your trust in God. The one thing it can't do is solve anything.

When worry creeps into your mind, ask God to help you figure out what you can control and what only God can control. Take action where you need to, and then readjust your focus. God's love and power are bigger than any hard times that may come your way.

ONE FINAL THOUGHT

Worry makes troubles look bigger and God look smaller, but turning your worries into prayers can help you do your job while letting God do his.

TIMELESS WISDOM FOR EVERYDAY LIVING

Refocusing on Reality

If you spend your whole life waiting for the storm, you'll never enjoy the sunshine.

Horace

Anxiety does not empty tomorrow of its sorrow—only today of its strength.

Charles Haddon Spurgeon

Be patient and wait for the LORD to act; don't be worried about those who prosper or those who succeed in their evil plans. Don't give in to worry or anger; it only leads to trouble.

Psalm 37:7–8 GNT

God cares for you, so turn all your worries over to him.

1 Peter 5:7 CEV

Worry weighs a person down; an encouraging word cheers a person up.

Proverbs 12:25 NLT

JESUS SPEAKS

Anxiety comes from strain, and strain is caused by too complete a dependence on ourselves, on our own devices, our own plans, our own idea of what we are able to do. Thomas Merton

I said, "I am falling"; but your constant love, O LORD, held me up. Whenever I am anxious and worried, you comfort me and make me glad.
Psalm 94:18–19 GNT

Much that worries us beforehand can afterward, quite unexpectedly, have a happy and simple solution. Worries just don't matter. Things really are in a better hand than ours.
Dietrich Bonhoeffer

To carry care to bed is to sleep with a pack on your back.
Thomas Haliburton

The Right Stuff

Peter answered, "I will never leave you, even though all the rest do!" Jesus said to Peter, "I tell you that before the rooster crows two times tonight, you will say three times that you do not know me."
MARK 14:29–30 GNT

THE STORY BEHIND WHAT JESUS SAID

The disciples joined Jesus in singing a hymn, but inwardly they were confused and frightened. They'd just finished the Passover meal, where Jesus had talked about betrayal and death. They'd seen Judas hurriedly leave the room. Now Jesus was saying they'd all desert him.

Peter jumped to his own defense. Peter knew how strong his love was for Jesus, but he didn't realize how weak he could be in the face of peer pressure. That very night, Peter denied knowing Jesus, even challenging God to strike him dead if he were lying, to convince those listening of his innocence. When put to the test, Peter's fear—of being arrested and of what others might think—proved momentarily stronger than his love for Jesus.

REFLECTIONS ON THE WORDS OF JESUS

Every single day, your actions announce whether you are choosing to honor or deny God. The fear of what others might think may push you to make a choice you know is a poor one.

There are times when following God means choosing to stand alone in a crowd, such as declining to join in when friends start to gossip or refusing to exceed the speed limit, even when your passengers are egging you on. Standing strong takes courage and a commitment to let God's opinion carry more weight than the opinions of those around you, even those of your closest friends.

Standing strong against peer pressure means fighting your battles before they start. Remind yourself each morning whose opinion matters most to you. Ask God to give you the right words to say if you find yourself in a confrontational situation. Choose carefully whom you'll spend time with. Thank God for your victories and ask his forgiveness when you fail. Dare to do what you know is right.

ONE FINAL THOUGHT

When God's opinion matters most to you, peer pressure will lose its power over you—freeing you to do what's right, no matter who's watching.

TIMELESS WISDOM FOR EVERYDAY LIVING

The Right Stuff

We should have great peace if we did not busy ourselves with what others say and do.

Thomas à Kempis

Knowing what is right is like deep water in the heart; a wise person draws from the well within.

Proverbs 20:5 THE MESSAGE

Even if you have to suffer for doing good things, God will bless you. So stop being afraid and don't worry about what people might do. Honor Christ and let him be the Lord of your life.

1 Peter 3:14–15a CEV

One with God is a majority.
William Carey

Every human being is intended to have a character of his own; to be what no other is, and to do what no other can do.

William Ellery Channing

Jesus said, "You are in for trouble when everyone says good things about you. That is what your own people said about those prophets who told lies." Luke 6:26 CEV

We are so much accustomed to disguise ourselves to others, that at length we disguise ourselves to ourselves.
François de La Rochefoucauld

What I want is God's approval! Am I trying to be popular with people? If I were still trying to do so, I would not be a servant of Christ.
Galatians 1:10a GNT

Never tire of doing what is right. 2 Thessalonians 3:13b NIV

Rock On

Jesus said, "Though the rain comes in torrents and the floodwaters rise and the winds beat against that house, it won't collapse, because it is built on rock."
MATTHEW 7:25 NLT

THE STORY BEHIND WHAT JESUS SAID

In Israel, it's rare for rain to fall between May and October. When the rainy season does arrive, sudden downpours can turn dry ditches into raging rivers, capable of washing away anything in their path—including houses. A house may look secure during the summer, but the winter storms reveal whether its foundation rests on sand that can shift or solid rock that will hold steady.

As Jesus finished what became known as the Sermon on the Mount, he challenged the large crowd to live what they'd learned. He reminded them that hard times would reveal what their lives were really built on, the solid rock of his teachings or the shaky sand of their own faulty wisdom.

REFLECTIONS ON THE WORDS OF JESUS

When you graduate from high school, you'll know a lot. Things like algebraic equations, conjugations for Spanish verbs, and examples of iambic pentameter will fill your brain. What will happen to all this knowledge ten years from now? Chances are that if you don't use it you'll lose much of it.

The same is true when you learn life lessons from God. Listening to what God says is a great first step. Taking what you know and applying it to what you do is how truth comes alive in your heart. It is what turns a knowledgeable person into a wise one.

You can get older without getting wiser, by building your life on a shaky foundation. God has given you all you need to stand strong in any situation. Making wise decisions about your relationships, your responsibilities, and your future begins with living what you're learning.

ONE FINAL THOUGHT

Wise people take what they've learned from God and move it from their head to their hearts by putting it into practice in their lives.

TIMELESS WISDOM FOR EVERYDAY LIVING

Rock On

Whoever walks with the wise becomes wise, but the companion of fools suffers harm.

Proverbs 13:20 NRSV

Common sense suits itself
to the ways of the world.
Wisdom tries to conform to
the ways of heaven.

Joseph Joubert

*Those who are wise—the
people of God—shall shine
as brightly as the sun's bril-
liance, and those who turn
many to righteousness will
glitter like stars forever.*

Daniel 12:3 TLB

Wisdom is the right use of knowledge.

Charles Haddon Spurgeon

Iron rusts from disuse; stagnant
water loses its purity and in
cold weather becomes frozen;
even so does inaction sap the
vigor of the mind.

Leonardo da Vinci

Obey God's message! Don't fool yourselves by just listening to it. If you hear the message and don't obey it, you are like people who stare at themselves in a mirror and forget what they look like as soon as they leave.

James 1:22–24 CEV

Wise people act in keeping with the knowledge they have. But foolish people show how foolish they are.

Proverbs 13:16 NIRV

We are not made righteous by doing righteous deeds; but when we have been made righteous we do righteous deeds.

Martin Luther

Knowing is not enough, we must apply. Willing is not enough, we must do. Johann von Goethe

Across Enemy Lines

Jesus said, "I'm telling you to love your enemies. Let them bring out the best in you, not the worst. When someone gives you a hard time, respond with the energies of prayer, for then you are working out of your true selves, your God-created selves."
MATTHEW 5:44b—45a
THE MESSAGE

THE STORY BEHIND WHAT JESUS SAID

When Jesus told the crowds to love their neighbor, he was repeating what God said in the Old Testament. Jewish religious leaders, however, had taught the crowds that their neighbor included only a fellow Jew or anyone who returned their love.

As Jesus explained that even a person's enemies were included in the category of "neighbor," the crowds grew understandably uncomfortable. The Pharisees taught that hating your enemies was totally acceptable. Jesus said the exact opposite. When Jesus spoke about love, he used a word that meant reaching out to others regardless of how you feel inside. This kind of *agape* love is not motivated by emotion but by the desire to do what's best for someone else.

REFLECTIONS ON THE WORDS OF JESUS

Loving others is easy—as long as they love you. However, when someone rubs you the wrong way, or just seems to dislike you for one reason or another, love doesn't come naturally. It can only happen supernaturally.

That's why it's important to pray for the people in your life. The supernatural power of your prayer works in three ways. It invites God to work through circumstances in the situation, to work in your enemy's heart, and to change your own heart toward that person.

God may nudge you to reach out with loving actions or words toward the one you're having difficulties with. This doesn't guarantee that your enemy will become your friend. However, that's not the point. God simply asks you to follow Jesus' example by loving others well. As your own heart softens toward those who are hard on you, your loving response demonstrates God's power to a watching world.

ONE FINAL THOUGHT

Praying for the people in your life with whom you have difficulty is the first step toward loving them as Jesus does.

TIMELESS WISDOM FOR EVERYDAY LIVING

Across Enemy Lines

In Jesus and for Him, enemies and friends alike are to be loved. Thomas à Kempis

Love for our neighbor consists of three things: to desire the greater good of everyone; to do what good we can when we can; to bear, excuse, and hide others' faults.

Jean Viannes

Don't be hateful and insult people just because they are hateful and insult you. Instead, treat everyone with kindness.

1 Peter 3:9a CEV

When we please the LORD, even our enemies make friends with us.

Proverbs 6:7 CEV

The Bible tells us to love our neighbors, and also to love our enemies; probably because they are generally the same people.

G. K. Chesterton

Our Scriptures tell us that if you see your enemy hungry, go buy that person lunch, or if he's thirsty, get him a drink. Your generosity will surprise him with goodness. Don't let evil get the best of you; get the best of evil by doing good.

Romans 12:20–21 THE MESSAGE

The best way to destroy an enemy is to make him a friend.

Abraham Lincoln

Don't mistreat someone who has mistreated you. But try to earn the respect of others, and do your best to live at peace with everyone.

Romans 12:17–18 CEV

To return evil for good is devilish; to return good for good is human; to return good for evil is divine.

Alfred Plummer

It's All in the Attitude

Jesus said, "God is Spirit, and only by the power of his Spirit can people worship him as he really is."
JOHN 4:24 GNT

THE STORY BEHIND WHAT JESUS SAID

Where to worship God was a controversial subject between Jews and Samaritans. They each believed their choice was better than the other one's choice. Of course, a Jewish man speaking to a woman, and particularly a racially mixed Samaritan woman, was also controversial. However, that's just what Jesus was doing with the woman at the well.

The woman tried to pull Jesus into a debate about worship to steer him away from his probing questions about her personal life. Jesus turned the discussion back to what was really important—her individual response to God. Jesus wanted the woman to understand that anyone—regardless of race, sex, or background—was free to worship God. Location wasn't important. Attitude was important.

REFLECTIONS ON THE WORDS OF JESUS

Just like the woman at the well, people today are still debating over the "right" way to worship God. "Are the old ways still good, or should we try new things?" "Should we raise our hands, stand, sit, or kneel?" "Is it okay to make a profit from selling CDs of worship music?"

If Jesus were asked questions like these today, he might have the same response that he did to the woman at the well—attitude is what really matters. Worship is more than singing a song or giving money to your church, although those are ways of honoring God. Worship is responding honestly and with your whole heart to who God is.

God isn't confined to a human body. His Spirit is everywhere. That means you can worship God any time of day, anywhere you are. Every time you obey him, pray to him, praise him, or love someone more deeply because of him, you're worshiping God. A humble heart and the power of God's spirit are all you need to worship God well.

ONE FINAL THOUGHT

When your heart is right with God, worship is a natural outpouring of your love for him that spills over into everything you do.

TIMELESS WISDOM FOR EVERYDAY LIVING

It's All in the Attitude

With Jesus' help, let us continually offer our sacrifice of praise to God by proclaiming the glory of his name. Hebrews 13:15 NLT

This is adoration; not a difficult religious exercise, but an attitude of the soul.

Evelyn Underhill

Come, let us bow down in worship, let us kneel before the LORD our Maker; for he is our God and we are the people of his pasture, the flock under his care.

Psalm 95:6—7 NIV

The worship of God is not a rule of safety—it is an adventure of the spirit.

Alfred North Whitehead

Sing praise to the LORD; tell the wonderful things he has done. Be glad that we belong to him; let all who worship him rejoice! Go to the LORD for help, and worship him continually.

1 Chronicles 16:9–11 GNT

My question:
What are God-worshipers like?
Your answer:
Arrows aimed at
God's bull's-eye.

Psalm 25:12 THE MESSAGE

Offer yourselves as a living sacrifice to God, dedicated to his service and pleasing to him. This is the true worship that you should offer.

Romans 12:1 GNT

We may be truly said to worship God, though we lack perfection; but we cannot be said to worship Him if we lack sincerity. Stephen Charnock

Team Spirit Rules

Jesus said, "Father, I pray that they can be one. As you are in me and I am in you, I pray that they can also be one in us. Then the world will believe that you sent me."
JOHN 17:21 NCV

THE STORY BEHIND WHAT JESUS SAID

As Jesus finished the Passover meal, his eyes rested on his disciples. His death and resurrection would open the way for them to spend eternity with God. However, Jesus also knew that trouble lay ahead for his friends.

The tight-knit group of followers would soon become a growing church with people of different cultures, backgrounds, and temperaments all worshiping God together. If they could work together as a team their ministry would be more effective—and their uncommon unity would make an invisible God more visible to those around them.

REFLECTIONS ON THE WORDS OF JESUS

To be successful, a band needs more than talented musicians. It needs unity. If band members can't agree on what makes a good song, or if the drummer and lead guitarist battle over which instrument should be featured in the mix, the group can forget about making it big.

What's true for a band is true for any team member. Whether you're involved in sports, at church, or just as part of your family, working together successfully begins with finding common ground. Focus on what you agree on. Refuse to get sidetracked by arguments over minor details. Listen openly to others' opinions. Accept that you can't always have things your way. And do what Jesus did—pray for your team.

Just as a band requires a mix of different instruments, an effective team benefits from including people with different skills, temperaments, and backgrounds. With God's help, harmony can happen. Just add humility and prayer.

ONE FINAL THOUGHT

Unity doesn't require uniformity, just God's help in humbly working through any differences you have with others that might prevent you from reaching a common goal.

TIMELESS WISDOM FOR EVERYDAY LIVING

Team Spirit Rules

Great discoveries and achievements invariably involve the cooperation of many minds.

Alexander Graham Bell

No one has ever seen God. But if we love each other, God lives in us, and his love has been brought to full expression through us.

1 John 4:12 NLT

Live in harmony with each other. Don't try to act important, but enjoy the company of ordinary people. And don't think you know it all!

Romans 12:16 NLT

How wonderful it is, how pleasant, for God's people to live together in harmony! Psalm 133:1 GNT

We are all one body, we have the same Spirit, and we have all been called to the same glorious future.

Ephesians 4:4 NLT

May the God who gives endurance and encour-agement give you a spirit of unity among your-selves as you follow Christ Jesus, so that with one heart and mouth you may glorify the God and Father of our Lord Jesus Christ.

Romans 15:5–6 NIV

If we focus on our differences, our focus is on each other. If we focus with unity, our focus is on God.

Author Unknown

Form all together one choir, so that, with the symphony of our feel-ings and having all taken the tone of God, you may sing with one voice to the Father through Jesus Christ.

Saint Ignatius of Antioch

It is by loving and being loved that one can come nearest to the soul of another. George MacDonald

The Yoke's on You

Jesus said, "Let me teach you, because I am humble and gentle, and you will find rest for your souls. For my yoke fits perfectly, and the burden I give you is light."
MATTHEW 11:29b–30 NLT

THE STORY BEHIND WHAT JESUS SAID

When Jesus talked about yokes and heavy burdens, oxen would most likely come to the minds of his listeners. Oxen were valuable in the farming society of Israel. Often paired together, they wore wooden yokes to plow fields, thresh corn, and transport heavy loads.

In the religious teachings of the Jews, men were said to be "yoked" to the Torah. In other words, they had to carry around all of the Old Testament laws, as well as the Pharisees' additional rules, wherever they went. When Jesus promised rest, he didn't offer to remove the yokes of those listening, making their lives burden free. Instead, Jesus offered his listeners a new way of life—a perfect yoke they could carry without becoming tired and overburdened.

REFLECTIONS ON THE WORDS OF JESUS

Picture yourself putting on your backpack filled with this semester's textbooks. Next add your best friend's textbooks, a couple of teacher's manuals, and your family's dirty laundry. Chances are that if you were carrying this backpack some-where other than your mind, the seams and straps—not to mention your back—would be ready to give out. That's because you're carrying much more than the backpack or you were designed to carry.

Something similar happens all too often in real life. You pick up a few worries, a too-hectic schedule, throw in a little guilt or the need to please everyone. Soon, you can hardly walk under the strain. You feel exhausted physically, mentally, emo-tionally, and spiritually.

God offers you rest. He never asks you to carry more than you and he can handle together. His healing, peace, and comfort provide a constant source of retreat and renewal, available free of charge. Check the yoke you're wearing. God's yoke always fits just right.

ONE FINAL THOUGHT

When life weighs heavy on your heart, turn to God for rest, asking him to help you unload anything you should never have picked up in the first place.

TIMELESS WISDOM FOR EVERYDAY LIVING

The Yoke's on You

The LORD lifts the burdens of those bent beneath their loads. Psalm 146:8b NLT

When the soul gives up all for love, so that it can have him that is all, then it finds true rest. Julian of Norwich

This is what the Sovereign LORD, the Holy One of Israel, says: "In repentance and rest is your salvation, in quietness and trust is your strength."

Isaiah 30:15a NIV

If He bids us carry a burden, He carries it also. Charles Spurgeon

Pile your troubles on God's shoulders—he'll carry your load, he'll help you out.

Psalm 55:22a THE MESSAGE

The love of God is this, that we obey His commandments. And His commandments are not burdensome, for whatever is born of God conquers the world. And this is the victory that conquers the world, our faith. 1 John 5:3–4 NRSV

Any concern too small to be turned into a prayer is too small to be made into a burden.
Corrie ten Boom

Ask where the good way is, and walk in it, and you will find rest for your souls.
Jeremiah 6:16 NIV

Cast all your cares on God; that anchor holds. Alfred, Lord Tennyson

Heart Check

Jesus said, "Whatever is in your heart determines what you say. A good person produces good words from a good heart."
MATTHEW 12:34b—35a NLT

THE STORY BEHIND WHAT JESUS SAID

The Pharisees were condemning Jesus' latest miracle. A man who had been blind and mute could now see and speak. The religious leaders, however, claimed that all they could see was Satan's power working through a false prophet. Jesus focused on trying to open the religious leaders' eyes.

Jesus spoke about how the health of a tree can be seen in its fruit. A healthy tree produces good, wholesome fruit. A sickly one produces fruit no one wants to eat. The same is true of a sick, unhealthy heart. It produces evil, cutting words. The Pharisees couldn't hide a good or an evil heart. Their words revealed their true nature.

REFLECTIONS ON THE WORDS OF JESUS

During a medical exam, your doctor listens to your heart to help determine if you're healthy. Determining your spiritual health also involves listening to your heart, only you don't need a stethoscope. All you need to do is listen to what comes out of your mouth.

Words that gossip, lie, cut others down, explode in anger, or tell whispered jokes are words that hurt—you, those around you, and God. You can't have a spiritually healthy heart by just trying to clean up your speech. It works the other way around. God's Spirit has to help clean up your heart.

Ask for God's help in becoming more aware of your words. Then dig a little deeper. Why do you say what you do? Are you angry? Embarrassed? Jealous? Trying to impress someone? Only God's Spirit can help you deal with your heart problems. As your motives and attitudes change, so will the kind of verbal fruit you'll be able to offer others.

ONE FINAL THOUGHT

What you say reveals what's hidden in your heart—so listen to yourself and learn, letting God's Spirit clean up your speech from the inside out.

TIMELESS WISDOM
FOR EVERYDAY LIVING

Heart Check

The LORD searches every heart and understands every motive behind the thoughts.

1 Chronicles 28:9b NIV

God has given us two ears, but one tongue, to show that we should be swift to hear, but slow to speak.

Thomas Watson

I will give you a new heart with new and right desires, and I will put a new spirit in you. I will take out your stony heart of sin and give you a new, obedient heart.

Ezekiel 36:26 NLT

Do your utmost to guard your heart, for out of it comes life. Walter Hilton

Our actions disclose what goes on within us, just as its fruit makes known a tree otherwise unknown to us.

Thalassios the Libyan

JESUS SPEAKS

Keep vigilant watch over your heart; that's where life starts. Don't talk out of both sides of your mouth; avoid careless banter, white lies, and gossip. Proverbs 4:23–24 THE MESSAGE

May the words of my mouth and the meditation of my heart be pleasing in your sight, O LORD, my Rock and my Redeemer.

Psalm 19:14 NIV

People who think they are religious but say things they should not say are just fooling themselves. Their "religion" is worth nothing.

James 1:26 NCV

Our words are a faithful index of the state of our souls.

Saint Francis de Sales

Moved to Action

Jesus called his
disciples to him
and said, "I have
compassion for
these people; they
have already been
with me three
days and have
nothing to eat."
MARK 8:2 NIV

THE STORY BEHIND WHAT JESUS SAID

Four thousand followers, many of them not Jewish, were
ready to head home. Though their spiritual hunger had
been satisfied, Jesus noticed that their physical hunger had
not. He felt compassion for them.

Apparently Jesus' disciples had very short memories.
They'd seen Jesus solve this problem before, but now they
were unsure what to do. As before, Jesus fed the crowd with
a few loaves of bread and small fish. But this time, instead
of having eleven small baskets of leftovers, they filled seven
spyris—baskets large enough to hold a man—making it a
day neither the crowd nor the disciples could forget.

REFLECTIONS ON THE WORDS OF JESUS

God has a lot of big things to be concerned about. War. Poverty. Abuse. Murder. Disease. Earthquakes. Evil, in general. Does he really care about your English final? Problems with your boyfriend or girlfriend? Your disappointment over not making the track team?

God cares about every detail of your life. Jesus didn't feed all of those people just to demonstrate God's power. He also did it because people were hungry. He took action because he could put himself in the shoes of the people around him. That's what having compassion is all about.

Compassion is a big part of learning to love others as Jesus did. It is more than having pity on someone. It is feeling so deeply what someone else is going through that you're moved to do something to alleviate their suffering. Open your eyes to the pain of those around you today, and then allow God to touch others' lives through you.

ONE FINAL THOUGHT

You can be Jesus' hands and feet in today's world by consciously putting yourself in a hurting person's shoes and letting compassion inspire you to action.

TIMELESS WISDOM
FOR EVERYDAY LIVING

Moved to Action

Whatever God does, the first outburst is always compassion. Meister Eckhart

As God's chosen people, holy and dearly loved, clothe yourselves with compassion.
Colossians 3:12a NIV

Remember, O LORD, your unfailing love and compassion, which you have shown from long ages past. Forgive the rebellious sins of my youth; look instead through the eyes of your unfailing love, for you are merciful, O LORD. Psalm 25:6–7 NLT

The dew of compassion is a tear. Lord Byron

By compassion we make others' misery our own, and so, by relieving them, we relieve ourselves also.
Thomas Browne

Praise be to the God and Father of our Lord Jesus Christ, the Father of compassion and the God of all comfort, who comforts us in all our troubles, so that we can comfort those in any trouble with the comfort we ourselves have received from God. 2 Corinthians 1:3–4 NIV

Compassion means that if I see my friend and my enemy in equal need, I shall help both equally.

Mechtilde of Magdeburg

The LORD is like a father to his children, tender and compassionate to those who fear him. For he understands how weak we are.
Psalm 103:13–14a NLT

The Lord is full of compassion and mercy. James 5:11b NIV

True Contentment

Jesus said, "You're blessed when you're content with just who you are—no more, no less. That's the moment you find yourselves proud owners of everything that can't be bought."

MATTHEW 5:5 THE MESSAGE

THE STORY BEHIND WHAT JESUS SAID

The Beatitudes, or the Blessings, are some of Jesus' most famous words. Each beatitude describes how when people bless God through a certain attitude or action he blesses them in return.

The Beatitude in Matthew 5:5 is traditionally translated as "Blessed are the meek, for they will inherit the earth." Jesus spoke these words to his disciples at the height of his popularity. As the crowds continued to grow, the disciples must have felt pretty important to have been chosen to accompany such a celebrity. Jesus was reminding them that popularity, power, or riches were not the key to contentment. Only the meek, those who are content to be exactly who God designed them to be, would find true contentment.

REFLECTIONS ON THE WORDS OF JESUS

Discontent feels a little like having the munchies. You search through the pantry and fridge, looking for the perfect snack that will make you feel satisfied. Passing up fruit, rice cakes, lunchmeat, yogurt, crackers, and string cheese, you come to the only logical conclusion . . . there is absolutely nothing to eat in this house.

It doesn't matter whether it's food, fame, a wad of cash, or a brand-new dirt bike, absolutely nothing can fill that hunger you have inside that drives you to want more. Nothing, that is, except God.

Discontent is a gift from heaven. The more it drives you to recognize that God is what you're really hungry for, the more contented you'll be. As you learn to appreciate what God has already given you, including the unique way he created you, you can begin to relax and enjoy exactly where—and who—you are.

ONE FINAL THOUGHT

You'll never feel you have enough in life until you find that enjoying God—and who he has created you to be—is the only thing your heart really craves.

TIMELESS WISDOM FOR EVERYDAY LIVING

True Contentment

God has two dwellings: one in heaven, and the other in a meek and thankful heart. Izaak Walton

You must keep all earthly treasures out of your heart, and let Christ be your treasure, and let him have your heart. Charles Spurgeon

Till you can sing and rejoice and delight in God as misers do in gold, and kings in scepters, you can never enjoy the world. Thomas Traherne

[God] satisfies me with the good things I long for. Psalm 103:5a NIRV

Whatever I have, wherever I am, I can make it through anything in the One who makes me who I am.

Philippians 4:13 THE MESSAGE

[The LORD says,] "Why spend money on what does not satisfy? Why spend your wages and still be hungry? Listen to me and do what I say, and you will enjoy the best food of all." Isaiah 55:2 GNT

When we cannot find contentment in ourselves it is useless to seek it elsewhere.

François de La Rochefoucauld

The heart is rich when it is content, and it is always content when its desires are fixed on God.

Miguel Febres Cordero-Munzo

Delight yourself in the LORD and he will give you the desires of your heart. Psalm 37:4 NIV

Catching a Vision

Jesus said to Simon, "Push out into deep water, and let down the nets for a catch. . . ." When they had done so, they caught such a large number of fish that their nets began to break.

LUKE 5:4–6 NIV

THE STORY BEHIND WHAT JESUS SAID

Fishing was Simon Peter's life. He'd grown up watching fishermen working on the Sea of Galilee in his hometown of Bethsaida, which means Fishtown. Peter made his living netting fish, and he had just spent the whole night working. He caught absolutely nothing.

When a teacher named Jesus—who was not even a fellow fisherman—directed Peter to try again, Peter acted. Peter had already seen Jesus miraculously heal his mother-in-law. Peter saw that Jesus not only cared about life-and-death situations, but he also cared about everyday concerns, like fishing. A miraculous catch of fish inspired Peter to leave everything he knew behind. Peter recognized that Jesus and his directions were worth following, no matter where they might lead.

JESUS SPEAKS

REFLECTIONS ON THE WORDS OF JESUS

As you look down the road toward graduation, some big decisions lay ahead: whether to specialize, where to go to school, where to live, whom to marry. . . . The direction you decide on will play a big part in determining what your future will look like.

God can help. He can move you beyond just making good decisions toward choosing the very best in life. This applies to life-changing decisions as well as to the smaller decisions you make every day.

When you're faced with a decision, do more than weigh the pros and cons. Weigh your choices against God's Word. See how your options line up with the guidelines on good living that God has provided. Ask for advice from people whose lives reflect their own close relationship with God. Ask God for a clear understanding of which way he wants you to go. Then make your choice and move forward, trusting God to guide you toward his best.

ONE FINAL THOUGHT

When it comes to choosing a direction, God guides you through his Word, the words of others, and the reassuring whisper of his Spirit in your heart.

TIMELESS WISDOM FOR EVERYDAY LIVING

Catching a Vision

If you are not guided by God you will be guided by someone or something else. Eric Liddell

If we are living now by the Holy Spirit, let us follow the Holy Spirit's leading in every part of our lives.

Galatians 5:25 NLT

Turn to me and have mercy on me, as you always do to those who love your name. Direct my footsteps according to your word; let no sin rule over me.

Psalm 119:132–133 NIV

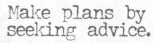

Make plans by seeking advice.

Proverbs 20:18a NIV

If God gives you a watch, are you honoring him more by asking him what time it is or by simply consulting the watch?

A. W. Tozer

Show me the path where I should walk, O LORD; point out the right road for me to follow. Lead me by your truth and teach me, for you are the God who saves me. All day long I put my hope in you. Psalm 25:4–5 NLT

The LORD says, "I will guide you along the best pathway for your life. I will advise you and watch over you." Psalm 32:8 NLT

I am satisfied that when the Almighty wants me to do or not to do any particular thing, he finds a way of letting me know.
Abraham Lincoln

When God shuts a door, He opens a window. John Ruskin

Living Your Priorities

> The Lord answered her,
> "Martha, Martha, you are
> worried and upset about
> many things. Only one
> thing is important."
> LUKE 10:41–42a NCV

THE STORY BEHIND WHAT JESUS SAID

The pressure of preparing the evening meal weighed heavily on Martha. But while Martha worked, her sister, Mary, listened to Jesus teach.

When Jesus spoke to Martha, he wasn't upset. He described Martha as *periespato*, meaning "distracted." What Martha was doing *for* Jesus was actually drawing her *away from* Jesus. Martha was more concerned that Mary wasn't helping than she was about not sitting at Jesus' feet herself. Details, like making dinner, were still important. Jesus simply longed for a relationship with Martha more than anything else— and he wanted Martha to long for that same thing.

REFLECTIONS ON THE WORDS OF JESUS

As you grow, so do your priorities. When you were a toddler, your main priority was to have a fun day. As a teen, your priorities expand to include doing your best at school, loving your friends and family well, and strengthening your relationship with God.

The more priorities you take on in life, the more difficult it gets to keep them in balance. Distractions—such as being offered last-minute concert tickets when you need to study for geometry—constantly tug at your schedule, threatening to pull it off balance.

Maintaining that balance begins with maintaining your focus. Know what your priorities are. If God asks you to do your work with excellence and your top priority is to please God, passing up those concert tickets is a no-brainer. Pray each morning for wisdom in knowing what to do and what to leave undone. When an opportunity arises, consider it in light of your priorities before making a commitment.

ONE FINAL THOUGHT

Asking God to help you understand what your true priorities are, then evaluating opportunities in light of those priorities, will help keep your life in balance.

TIMELESS WISDOM FOR EVERYDAY LIVING

Living Your Priorities

Jesus said, "Put God's kingdom first. Do what he wants you to do." Matthew 6:33a NIRV

Our purpose is to please God, not people. He is the one who examines the motives of our hearts.

1 Thessalonians 2:4b NLT

Where no plan is laid, where the disposal of time is surrendered merely to the chance of incident, chaos will soon reign.

Victor Hugo

The soul that has no established aim loses itself.

Michel de Montaigne

In everything you do, put God first, and he will direct you and crown your efforts with success. **Proverbs 3:6** TLB

Is the Holy Spirit your companion? Has Christ been gentle and loving toward you? Then make my joy complete by agreeing with each other. Have the same love. Be one in spirit and purpose. Philippians 2:1b-2 NIRV

Obstacles are those frightening things you see when you take your eyes off the goal.
Hannah More

I want you to do whatever will help you serve the Lord best, with as few distractions as possible.
1 Corinthians 7:35a NLT

A good archer is not known by his arrows but his aim. Thomas Fuller

In God's Chat Room

Jesus said, "When you pray, don't babble on and on as people of other religions do. They think their prayers are answered only by repeating their words again and again."
MATTHEW 6:7 NLT

THE STORY BEHIND WHAT JESUS SAID

Jesus often went off by himself to pray. To help his followers better understand what he was doing in private, Jesus gave the crowds a few guidelines to follow.

Many people prayed to idols, repeating the same words over and over. They believed that the more they repeated their magic spell, the more likely it was that the gods would grant their request. The Jews prayed to the only true God, but sometimes they mindlessly repeated their prayers out of habit. Jesus explained that the sincerity of the heart behind a prayer is more important than the actual words being said.

REFLECTIONS ON THE WORDS OF JESUS

Like a good friend whom you've just seen at school but who calls you up the minute you get home to catch up on your day, God invites you to share what's up with him. Anything that's important to you is important to God.

Prayer is simply talking to God about what matters. Just share with God like you would a good friend. Tell him what you're worried about, fearful of, ecstatic over, or thankful for. Ask him for what you need. It's true that he already knows, but talking to him about it invites God to act. When you're finished speaking, take time to sit quietly, listening for God's response.

Don't hesitate to pray for the same thing more than once. The Bible encourages persistence in prayer. Just be careful that your persistence doesn't deteriorate into thoughtlessly repeating words that no longer mean anything to you. Just share what's on your heart anytime, anywhere, every day.

ONE FINAL THOUGHT

Prayer can be a heartfelt delight when you share what honestly matters to you with the one who knows you best.

TIMELESS WISDOM FOR EVERYDAY LIVING

In God's Chat Room

When a believing person prays, great things happen. James 5:16b NCV

My heart has heard you say,
"Come and talk with me."
And my heart responds,
"LORD, I am coming."

Psalm 27:8 NLT

True prayers are like those carrier pigeons which find their way so well; they cannot fail to go to heaven, for it is from heaven that they came; they are only going home.

Charles Spurgeon

Prayer is keeping company with God.

Clement of Alexandria

We talk about heaven being so far away. It is within speaking distance to those who belong there.

Dwight Moody

JESUS SPEAKS

Listen to my words, O LORD, and hear my sighs. Listen to my cry for help, my God and king! I pray to you, O LORD; you hear my voice in the morning; at sunrise I offer my prayer and wait for your answer. Psalm 5:1–3 GNT

Prayer is the key of heaven; faith is the hand that turns it.

Thomas Watson

There is not in the world a kind of life more sweet and delightful than that of a continual conversation with God.

Brother Lawrence

Always be joyful and never stop praying. 1 Thessalonians 5:16–17 CEV

"Obey" Isn't a Four-Letter Word

Jesus said, "Why were you looking for me? Didn't you know that I had to be here, dealing with the things of my Father?" But [his parents] had no idea what he was talking about. So he went back to Nazareth with them, and lived obediently with them.

LUKE 2:49–51a THE MESSAGE

THE STORY BEHIND WHAT JESUS SAID

The religious teachers who'd gathered in the Temple sat quietly, astonished at the questions, answers, and religious understanding they were hearing. Most astonishing of all was the fact that these words came from twelve-year-old Jesus.

When, after a frantic search, Jesus' parents finally found him, the boy's explanation as to why he hadn't headed home with his family was that he was doing what his Father wanted. Even at twelve, Jesus recognized that his relationship with God was different from that of other people—that God had something uniquely important for him to do. However, Jesus put his valid reasons for pride aside. He humbled himself, choosing to honor his heavenly Father by obeying his earthly parents.

REFLECTIONS ON THE WORDS OF JESUS

The older you get, the less dependent you become on the adults who have cared for you as you've grown. Once you hit your teens, you're old enough to feed yourself, wash your own clothes, perhaps even drive yourself to school. However, God still has a few lessons for you to learn before you're totally out on your own. One is to value your parents. They're not perfect, but they are worthy of your love, honor, and obedience.

God knows your family situation. Regardless of whether your parents are lenient or strict, whether they believe in God or not, God has put them in a place of authority over you. Your respect is a gift God asks you to give them. Honoring your parents' words and requests with your obedience takes humility. Look to Jesus for your example. By honoring your parents, you're honoring God.

ONE FINAL THOUGHT

Being obedient to your parents in both actions and attitude not only honors them but also honors your Father in heaven.

TIMELESS WISDOM FOR EVERYDAY LIVING

"Obey" Isn't a Four-Letter Word

Follow God's example in everything you do, because you are his dear children.

Ephesians 5:1 NLT

When home is ruled according to God's Word, angels might be asked to stay with us, and they would not find themselves out of their element.

Charles Spurgeon

Obedience means marching right on whether we feel like it or not. Many times we go against our feelings. Faith is one thing, feeling is another.

Dwight Moody

Obedience is the key to every door.

George MacDonald

Home is a mighty test of character. What you are at home you are everywhere, whether you demonstrate it or not.

Thomas De Witt Talmage

You belong to the Lord, and you do the right thing when you obey your parents. The first commandment with a promise says, "Obey your father and your mother, and you will have a long and happy life." Ephesians 6:1-3 CEV

Intelligent children listen to their parents; foolish children do their own thing.
Proverbs 13:1 THE MESSAGE

My child, pay attention to what your father and mother tell you. Their teaching will improve your character as a handsome turban or a necklace improves your appearance.

Proverbs 1:8 GNT

Obey your parents in all things, because this pleases the Lord.
Colossians 3:20 NCV

Oops!

Jesus said to Peter, "Put your sword back into its sheath. Shall I not drink from the cup the Father has given me?"
JOHN 18:11 NLT

THE STORY BEHIND WHAT JESUS SAID

After the Passover meal, tension was running high. As Jesus and his eleven remaining disciples entered an olive grove, the glow of torches and lanterns broke through the darkness. Over six hundred soldiers and Temple guards stood before them. Out of loyalty and courage, mixed with fear and foolishness, Peter took the situation into his own hands.

Jesus reminded Peter that no matter how desperate things looked at that moment, the situation was in God's hands, not Peter's. Peter felt he was doing the right thing because he didn't understand the important job that God the Father had sent Jesus to do. But Jesus was not sidetracked from doing what his Father asked.

REFLECTIONS ON THE WORDS OF JESUS

When Peter lashed out with his sword, Jesus handled the consequences of Peter's actions. He healed Malchus's ear and then went forward with God's plan. Though God's Spirit is still close at hand today, chances are that the consequences of any impulsive decisions you make are not going to miraculously disappear. You're going to have to live with them.

When adrenaline is running high, especially if there's pressure to make a decision right away, it's easy to go with your emotions instead of waiting for God's wisdom. By taking matters into your own hands, however, even your good intentions can get in the way of good things God has planned.

When you're unsure of what to do, the first thing that pops into your mind isn't always the best. Take a moment to collect your thoughts and pray. If possible, put off making a decision until your emotions have cooled down. Trust God's Word and direction over your own fickle feelings.

ONE FINAL THOUGHT

Let all your decisions be thoughtful ones guided by careful consideration, godly wisdom, and biblical guidelines instead of your emotions.

TIMELESS WISDOM FOR EVERYDAY LIVING

Oops!

Mixed motives twist life into tangles; pure motives take you straight down the road.
Proverbs 21:8a THE MESSAGE

Don't live carelessly, unthinkingly. Make sure you understand what the Master wants.
Ephesians 5:17 THE MESSAGE

Prepare your minds for action; be self-controlled; set your hope fully on the grace to be given you when Jesus Christ is revealed.
1 Peter 1:13 NIV

Hurry is the death of prayer.
Samuel Chadwick

Quiet waiting before God would save [us] from many a mistake and from many a sorrow. James Hudson Taylor

On every level of life from housework to height of prayer, in all judgment and all efforts to get things done, hurry and impatience are sure marks of an amateur. Evelyn Underhill

O Lord, may I be directed what to do and what to leave undone.

Elizabeth Fry

There is nothing so small but that we may honor God by asking his guidance of it, or insult him by taking it into our own hands.

John Ruskin

A person who moves too quickly may go the wrong way. Proverbs 19:2b NLT

Fear Isn't for the Birds

Jesus said, "Not even a sparrow, worth only half a penny, can fall to the ground without your Father knowing it. . . . So don't be afraid; you are more valuable to him than a whole flock of sparrows."
MATTHEW 10:29, 31 NLT

THE STORY BEHIND WHAT JESUS SAID

Sparrows were like today's macaroni-and-cheese for the poor in Palestine. When times were tight, the poorest of families would purchase an inexpensive sparrow and split it among themselves for dinner. By describing the active interest God took in the lives of common, seemingly worthless birds, Jesus contrasted how deeply God obviously cared about those who were so close to his heart.

Jesus had just finished speaking about how God's power was stronger than any evil one might face in life. Then he gave the crowd another reason to be unafraid—God's love was so great that nothing could happen to them without his knowledge. God was involved in even the smallest detail of their lives.

REFLECTIONS ON THE WORDS OF JESUS

When you move to a new address, you take special care packing what's valuable to you, especially if it's fragile. You wrap it carefully, protect it with padding, and write a bold HANDLE WITH CARE on the side of the box. You may even decide to personally carry it with you to make sure it arrives intact. You do everything in your power to make sure that it's not damaged, broken, or misplaced along the way.

As you travel toward your home in heaven, God is taking special care of you. You are priceless in his eyes, so he has stamped an invisible HANDLE WITH CARE on your life. God's power and care are limitless, ready to ease any fears that may arise on your journey.

Nothing can happen to you that God does not allow. That's an assurance that you and God together can handle anything that comes your way. Let that simple truth help you face, and conquer, your greatest fears.

ONE FINAL THOUGHT

No fear can stand up to the truth that God loves you so much that he won't allow anything into your life that he can't use for your good.

TIMELESS WISDOM FOR EVERYDAY LIVING

Fear Isn't for the Birds

The LORD is my light and my salvation—so why should I be afraid? Psalm 27:1a NLT

In his goodness he chose to make us his own children by giving us his true word. And we, out of all creation, became his choice possession.

James 1:18 NLT

Let us step into darkness and reach out for the hand of God. The path of faith and darkness is so much safer than the one we would choose by sight.

George MacDonald

Fear knocked at the door. Faith answered. And lo, no one was there. Author Unknown

One of the effects of fear is to disturb the senses and cause things to appear other than what they are.

Miguel de Cervantes

If I could hear Christ praying for me in the next room, I would not fear a million enemies. Yet distance makes no difference. He is praying for me. Robert Murray M'Cheyne

God loves you as though you are the only person in the world, and he loves everyone the way he loves you.

Saint Augustine of Hippo

We are God's master-piece. He has created us anew in Christ Jesus, so that we can do the good things he planned for us long ago.

Ephesians 2:10 NLT

Where God's love is, there is no fear, because God's perfect love drives out fear. 1 John 4:18a NCV

Memory Jogger

Jesus took some bread in his hands and gave thanks for it. He broke the bread and handed it to his apostles. Then he said, "This is my body, which is given for you. Eat this as a way of remembering me!"
LUKE 22:19 CEV

THE STORY BEHIND WHAT JESUS SAID

Like all devout Jews, the disciples drank wine and ate bread every year during Passover. Tonight, however, was different. Jesus called the bread his "body" and the wine his "blood."

After Jesus died on the cross, the old agreement between God and people changed. Priests no longer needed to sacrifice animals to gain God's temporary forgiveness. Through Jesus' sacrificial death, eternal forgiveness was available for every individual. This news was worth celebrating more often than once a year. That's why the Lord's Supper has been celebrated in churches around the world from the time of Jesus' resurrection right up to today.

REFLECTIONS ON THE WORDS OF JESUS

What Jesus did on the cross is hard to forget. It's not every day someone loves you so much he's willing to sacrifice his body and blood for you—and by doing so change your eternal destiny. Life gets busy. Schoolwork piles up. Plans for the prom or defensive basketball strategies clutter your mind. Taking part in the Lord's Supper helps you refocus on what's most important. Though different churches celebrate this time of remembrance in different ways, the "how" isn't what matters. It's the "why" that will fill your heart with thanks. In turn, that will lead to praising God and a desire to learn more about him.

That's one reason why becoming part of a local church where you can celebrate the Lord's Supper with other Christ followers is so important. What the Lord's Supper will help you remember, a church community will help you learn to apply to your life.

ONE FINAL THOUGHT

Being an active part of a local church will help remind you of what's truly important in life—who Jesus is and what he's done for you.

TIMELESS WISDOM FOR EVERYDAY LIVING

Memory Jogger

The church is not wood and stone, but the company of people who believe in Christ.

Martin Luther

Nothing lasts but the church.

George Herbert

Every time you eat this bread and drink this cup you are re-telling the message of the Lord's death, that he has died for you. Do this until he comes again.

1 Corinthians 11:26 TLB

Be careful that you do not forget the LORD.

Deuteronomy 6:12a NIV

Although the elements of the world crash against it and batter it, the church offers the safest harbour of salvation for all in distress.

Saint Ambrose

JESUS SPEAKS

Some people have gotten out of the habit of meeting for worship, but we must not do that. We should keep on encouraging each other, especially since you know that the day of the Lord's coming is getting closer. Hebrews 10:25 CEV

None understand better the nature of real distinction than those who have entered into unity. Johann Tauler

If Jesus Christ be God and died for me, then no sacrifice can be too great for me to make for him.

Charles Thomas Studd

The church is Christ's body, in which he speaks and acts, by which he fills everything with his presence. Ephesians 1:23b THE MESSAGE

One Life to Live

Peter asked Jesus, "Lord, what about him?" Jesus answered, "What is it to you, if I want him to live until I return? You must follow me."
JOHN 21:20 CEV

THE STORY BEHIND WHAT JESUS SAID

The night Jesus died, Peter denied knowing him—three times. Now Peter was face-to-face with his resurrected Messiah and undoubtedly feeling a little uncomfortable. Jesus asked Peter if he loved him—three times. As Jesus reinforced his own love for Peter, he also gave him an important job, taking care of the early church.

Instead of being concerned about his awesome new responsibility, Peter's main concern was over Jesus' best friend, John. Peter wanted to know what was going to happen to him. Would John's life make a greater impact than his own? Jesus responded with the same words he'd spoken when they first met: "Follow me." Peter's focus needed to be on Jesus instead of those around him.

REFLECTIONS ON THE WORDS OF JESUS

Although attending school may prevent you from getting hooked on television soap operas, junior high and high school can make you feel as though you're living in one. It is easy to get wrapped up in each other's lives. Who broke up with whom, who made the cheerleading squad and who didn't, who said what in the locker room.

Being involved in people's lives because you care about them is one thing. Trying to live their lives for them, or wishing you were in their shoes, is quite another. God has given you one life to live—your own.

When you take your eyes off God and focus on the lives of other people, it distracts you from God's unique purpose in your own life. It also leads to pride, jealousy, gossip, and even doubt about God's fairness and love. When your mind starts heading in that direction, change channels. Refocus on God and the direction he wants you to go.

ONE FINAL THOUGHT

Keeping your eyes on God and his unique plan for your future can help you avoid the destructive side effects that come from comparing your life with others.

TIMELESS WISDOM FOR EVERYDAY LIVING

One Life to Live

Do not look out only for yourselves. Look out for the good of others also. 1 Corinthians 10:24 NCV

Fix your attention on God. You'll be changed from the inside out. Readily recognize what he wants from you, and quickly respond to it. Romans 12:2b THE MESSAGE

No matter how significant you are, it is only because of what you are a part of.
1 Corinthians 12:19b THE MESSAGE

Before I judge my neighbor, let me walk a mile in his moccasins.
Sioux Proverbs

We awaken in others the same attitude of mind we hold toward them.
Elbert Hubbard

Make a careful exploration of who you are and the work you have been given, and then sink yourself into that. Don't be impressed with yourself. Don't compare yourself with others. Each of you must take responsibility for doing the creative best you can with your own life.

Galatians 6:4–5 THE MESSAGE

It is very easy to manage our neighbor's business, but our own sometimes bothers us. Josh Billings

We should have great peace if we did not busy ourselves with what others say and do.

Thomas à Kempis

The business of finding fault is very easy, and that of doing better very difficult. Saint Francis de Sales

Hot Stuff

Jesus said, "Carelessly call a brother 'idiot!' and you just might find yourself hauled into court. Thoughtlessly yell 'stupid!' at a sister and you are on the brink of hellfire."
MATTHEW 5:22b THE MESSAGE

THE STORY BEHIND WHAT JESUS SAID

The Jewish crowd listening to Jesus knew the Ten Commandments. They knew God said, "Don't murder." Jesus explained that God not only condemned murder, but he also condemned the anger that often led to it.

As Jesus talked about God's "court" judging their angry words, faces may have come to the minds of many of them. They were not only the faces of physical brothers and sisters, but they were also the faces of spiritual ones, people in God's family they'd felt bitterness toward. After making the crowd aware of their own murderous words, Jesus continued speaking, offering them hope for change.

REFLECTIONS ON THE WORDS OF JESUS

You've seen it on the big screen. The timer is counting down on a bomb that's ready to explode, and everyone is trying to remember exactly how to defuse the explosive device before it detonates. *Is it the red wire or the blue wire that you cut first?* In the land of movie make-believe, they always get it right.

In real life, you're faced with potential time bombs every day. Anytime someone cuts you down, inconveniences you, or just happens to catch you in a grumpy mood, that timer can start ticking. When it does, don't ignore it. Deal with the problem as soon as possible instead of letting emotions build up to disaster. Cut the appropriate verbal wires by being quick to listen to what others have to say and careful in your own response.

If a bomb has already gone off in a relationship, don't overlook the damage. Apologize, offer forgiveness, and with God's help, begin again.

ONE FINAL THOUGHT

Defusing anger by listening carefully, speaking thoughtfully, and reconciling quickly, when necessary, will prevent angry words and actions from killing relationships.

TIMELESS WISDOM FOR EVERYDAY LIVING

Hot Stuff

The LORD is compassionate and gracious, slow to anger, abounding in love. Psalm 103:8 NIV

However just your words, you spoil everything when you speak them with anger.

John Chrysostom

"Don't sin by letting anger gain control over you." Don't let the sun go down while you are still angry, for anger gives a mighty foothold to the Devil.

Ephesians 4:26–27 NLT

A gentle answer
quiets anger,
but a harsh
one stirs it up.

Proverbs 15:1 GNT

Speak when you are angry and you will make the best speech you will ever regret.

Ambrose Bierce

JESUS SPEAKS

My dear brothers and sisters, be quick to listen, slow to speak, and slow to get angry. Your anger can never make things right in God's sight.
James 1:19–20 NLT

There is no greater obstacle to the presence of the Spirit in us than anger.
John Climacus

Keep away from angry, short-tempered people, or you will learn to be like them and endanger your soul.
Proverbs 22:24 NLT

Anger is quieted by a gentle word just as fire is quenched by water.
Jean Pierre Camus

Enjoying Life's Wild Ride

Jesus said, "If you obey my commands, you will remain in my love. I have told you these things so that you can have the same joy I have and so that your joy will be the fullest possible joy."
JOHN 15:10b–11 NCV

THE STORY BEHIND WHAT JESUS SAID

It was Jesus' last night with his disciples. Jesus chose his last words to those he loved very carefully. Jesus knew the days ahead would be filled with intense ups and downs for those who followed him. His hope was that his disciples would stay strong and steady, joyfully holding tightly to the truth he'd taught them.

Though Jesus would no longer be close to them physically, Jesus explained to his disciples how they could remain close to him—the same way he remained close to his heavenly Father. Jesus explained that through obedience, the disciples' experience of God's love would deepen. That love would be a constant source of joy, no matter what circumstances they faced.

REFLECTIONS ON THE WORDS OF JESUS

Roller coasters are designed to take you on a wild ride. One minute you're elated at how high the coaster has climbed. The next your stomach feels as though it's dropping through the floorboards as you hurtle toward the ground. You can enjoy the experience because you know you're safe—as long as you remain in your seat.

Remaining in God is what allows you to fully enjoy the roller coaster ride of life. When you try to make life work on your own, it's easy to get hooked on the highs and fall to pieces during the lows. Your happiness ends up being dependent on your present circumstances.

Joy doesn't ride an emotional roller coaster. It helps you delight in God and life, regardless of your circumstances. Choose joy today by remaining in God's seat of safety. Believe what he says, do what he asks, and stay close to him in prayer, through all life's ups and downs.

ONE FINAL THOUGHT

Joy isn't found through favorable circumstances; joy is found by choosing to remain close to God and his love through obedience.

TIMELESS WISDOM
FOR EVERYDAY LIVING

Enjoying Life's Wild Ride

The joy that the Lord gives you will make you strong. Nehemiah 8:10b GNT

There is not one blade of grass, there is no color in this world that is not intended to make us rejoice.

John Calvin

Let us fix our eyes on Jesus, the author and perfecter of our faith, who for the joy set before him endured the cross.

Hebrews 12:2a NIV

Joy is the surest sign of the presence of God.

Pierre Teilhard de Chardin

This is the secret of joy. We shall no longer strive for our own way; but commit ourselves, easily and simply, to God's way. Evelyn Underhill

You have changed my sadness into a joyful dance; you have taken away my sorrow and surrounded me with joy. So I will not be silent; I will sing praise to you. LORD, you are my God; I will give you thanks forever.

Psalm 30:11–12 GNT

Till you can sing and rejoice and delight in God, as misers do in gold, and kings in scepters, you never enjoy the world.

Thomas Traherne

Christ is not only a remedy for your weariness and trouble, but he will give you an abundance of the contrary, joy and delight.

Jonathan Edwards

I will rejoice in the LORD, I will be joyful in God my Savior.

Habakkuk 3:18 NIV

The Little Guy

Jesus intervened: "Let the children alone, don't prevent them from coming to me. God's kingdom is made up of people like these."

MATTHEW 19:14
THE MESSAGE

THE STORY BEHIND WHAT JESUS SAID

Jesus was an important person, a current celebrity in the Jewish world. His disciples recognized how valuable Jesus' time was, so they tried to protect him from interruptions. Jesus, however, never treated people as interruptions, even people whom others viewed as insignificant.

Jesus took time to bless the children and pray for them. He made them feel important, because in God's eyes, that's exactly what they were. Jesus wanted the disciples to recognize that the kingdom of God's family did not just include people others looked up to. It also included those who were ignored or overlooked—the sick, the poor, the outcast, and the very young.

REFLECTIONS ON THE WORDS OF JESUS

You know who they are, the popular kids. Whether it's their athletic ability, charismatic personality, or natural good looks, somehow these individuals have ended up on a pedestal. At the opposite end of the scale are the kids everyone seems to make fun of, the so-called losers. If Jesus showed up at your school, whom do you think he'd hang out with?

Jesus chose to spend time with all kinds of people—Pharisees, tax collectors, fishermen, prostitutes, misfits, and your average, ordinary Joes and Janes. He encouraged people to notice widows, orphans, and the poor. Whoever was significant to his Father was significant to Jesus. That included every individual ever created.

It's easy to spend time with people you're naturally attracted to. Choosing to reach out to people who are easily overlooked takes a commitment to love like Jesus did. Ask God to give you that kind of love and the wisdom to know how to express it best.

ONE FINAL THOUGHT

To love others like Jesus did, you need to appreciate every individual's eternal significance, regardless of how unimportant a person may appear to be.

TIMELESS WISDOM FOR EVERYDAY LIVING

The Little Guy

Whatever a person may be like, we must still love them because we love God. John Calvin

It is much easier to preach the gospel of love for mankind than it is to love single, individual, not very lovable sinners.

William Barclay

My dear brothers and sisters, as believers in our glorious Lord Jesus Christ, never think some people are more important than others. James 2:1 NCV

Kindness is in our power, even when fondness is not. Samuel Johnson

Be friendly with everyone. Don't be proud and feel that you are smarter than others. Make friends with ordinary people. Romans 12:16 CEV

I'll call nobodies and make them somebodies; I'll call the unloved and make them beloved. In the place where they yelled out, "You're nobody!" they're calling you "God's living children."
Romans 9:25–26 THE MESSAGE

Let everyone be important in your eyes, and do not despise those whose knowledge is less than yours.
John of Apamea

Share the sorrow of those being mistreated, as though you feel their pain in your own bodies.
Hebrews 13:3b NLT

Be fair with everyone, and don't have any favorites. 1 Timothy 5:21b CEV

Words Worth Chewing On

The devil came to Jesus to tempt him, saying, "If you are the Son of God, tell these rocks to become bread." Jesus answered, "It is written in the Scriptures, 'A person does not live by eating only bread, but by everything God says.'"

MATTHEW 4:3-4 NCV

THE STORY BEHIND WHAT JESUS SAID

Jesus hadn't eaten in forty days. He was hungry, tired, and alone. That's when Satan came to test him, to see if Jesus would obey his Father, no matter what.

Considering how hungry Jesus was, turning stones into bread was tempting. After all, there was nothing really wrong with providing himself with some food—except that it was not his Father's plan. Jesus answered Satan's challenge by quoting a verse from the Old Testament. Satan quoted a verse right back at him. Satan knew Scripture, but he didn't obey it. Jesus knew that the true power of God's Word came from doing what it said.

REFLECTIONS ON THE WORDS OF JESUS

The Bible is more than good advice. It's food for your soul. It keeps you strong and helps you grow, like a serving of spiritual vegetables. While physically eating a balanced diet helps you fight off disease, mentally chewing on portions of Scripture helps you fight off the temptation to disobey God.

However, just as you wouldn't eat all the food you need for a year in one sitting, you can't digest the whole Bible all at once. It is best to eat small portions each day. Try reading a chapter from both the Old and New Testaments. Working your way through Psalms and the Gospels is a good place to start.

Use a study Bible to better understand what you're reading. Keep a journal of what God's teaching you. Ask him how to apply what you've read. Write down verses you want to remember, then read through them each day. Soon, those verses will easily come to mind when you need them most.

ONE FINAL THOUGHT

When it comes to fighting off the urge to go the wrong way, prepare yourself for battle ahead of time by reading the Bible every day.

TIMELESS WISDOM FOR EVERYDAY LIVING

Words Worth Chewing On

Nobody ever outgrows Scripture; the book widens and deepens with our years. Charles Spurgeon

How can a young person live a clean life? By carefully reading the map of your Word.

Psalm 119:9 THE MESSAGE

We must read the Bible through the eyes of shipwrecked people for whom everything has gone overboard.

Karl Barth

Taste and see that the LORD is good. Oh, the joys of those who trust in him!

Psalm 34:8 NLT

When you read God's word, you must constantly be saying to yourself, "It is talking to me, and about me." Søren Kierkegaard

Do not let this Book of the Law depart from your mouth; meditate on it day and night, so that you may be careful to do everything written in it. Then you will be prosperous and successful.

Joshua 1:8 NIV

Divine Scripture is the feast of wisdom, and the single books are the various dishes. Saint Ambrose

God's laws are perfect. They protect us, make us wise, and give us joy and light. God's laws are pure, eternal, just. They are more desirable than gold.

Psalm 19:7–10a TLB

The Bible is a letter God sent to us; prayer is a letter we send to him. Matthew Henry

Friends Till the End

Jesus said, "I command you to love each other in the same way that I love you. And here is how to measure it— the greatest love is shown when people lay down their lives for their friends."
JOHN 15:12–13 NLT

THE STORY BEHIND WHAT JESUS SAID

Jesus developed a close relationship with the twelve men who followed him. Now it was time to say good-bye. After Jesus watched Judas leave to betray him, Jesus told the eleven remaining disciples how much he loved them—one last time. Jesus was their Teacher, Messiah, and Lord, but their relationship was more intimate than teacher and student. Jesus also related to these men as friend to friend.

The next day, Jesus would show his love for his friends by sacrificing his life to save the lives of everyone he'd call friend throughout history. That night, Jesus challenged those he loved to love others as he had loved them—sacrificially.

REFLECTIONS ON THE WORDS OF JESUS

"What's in it for me?" is a popular way of analyzing relationships. You weigh what you expect to get with what you have to give up and see if the scales tip favorably in your direction. True friendship throws that scale out the window. Instead it asks, "How can I give of myself in love to you?"

Chances are, you'll never have a reason to physically lay down your life for a friend. However, every day you're faced with opportunities where you can choose to lay down what you value in life—your time, your energy, and your resources.

Choosing to meet someone else's needs at the expense of your own without asking for anything in return is when your gift of friendship most resembles the kind Jesus spoke of. Your job is to love your friends well by unselfishly sharing what you have, as well as who you are.

ONE FINAL THOUGHT

True friends help meet the needs of those they care about—as God leads them—by giving freely of their time, energy, resources, and love.

TIMELESS WISDOM FOR EVERYDAY LIVING

Friends Till the End

Give what you have. To someone, it may be better than you dare to think.
Henry Wadsworth Longfellow

Friends come and friends go, but a true friend sticks by you like family.
Proverbs 18:24 THE MESSAGE

A true friend . . . advises justly, assists readily, adventures boldly, takes all patiently, defends courageously, and continues a friend unchangeably.
William Penn

These God-chosen lives all around—what splendid friends they make!
Psalm 16:3 THE MESSAGE

Friendship consists in forgetting what one gives and remembering what one receives. Alexandre Dumas

Two are better off than one, because together they can work more effectively. If one of them falls down, the other can help him up. But if someone is alone and falls, it's just too bad, because there is no one to help him.

Ecclesiastes 4:9–10 GNT

Pursue faith and love and peace, and enjoy the companionship of those who call on the Lord with pure hearts.

2 Timothy 2:22b NLT

A true friend is the gift of God, and he only who made hearts can unite them.

Robert South

The only thing to do is to hug one's friend tight and do one's job.

Edith Wharton

On the Edge

Jesus fell face down on the ground. . . . "Abba, Father," he said, "everything is possible for you. Please take this cup of suffering away from me. Yet I want your will, not mine."
MARK 14:35a–36 NLT

THE STORY BEHIND WHAT JESUS SAID

With a heartfelt cry of *Abba* (which means "daddy" in Aramaic), Jesus ran straight to his Father's arms in prayer. Jesus knew his arrest and execution were close at hand. Anyone would want to escape the agony of crucifixion, but pain and death were not what Jesus feared. Jesus' agony was the thought of being separated from God.

As Jesus freely expressed the depth of his emotions, he also expressed the depth of his love. He voiced his acceptance of God's answer to his prayer, regardless of whether that answer meant suffering or relief.

REFLECTIONS ON THE WORDS OF JESUS

If a cavity has you moaning in pain, the dentist helps you by first causing you even more pain. Before beginning work, the dentist injects an anesthetic into your already sensitive gums. You submit to the suffering because you trust the dentist to know what is best. You trust this professional to have your best interest at heart.

When it comes to your best interest, no one knows you better than God. Yet sometimes he allows suffering to not only enter your life but push you to the edge. Suffering doesn't usually feel like it's in your best interest. Whether physical or emotional, pain of any kind still hurts—no matter what the reason.

When that happens, Jesus has shown you what to do. Honestly cry out to God. Ask your friends to pray for you. Then trust and accept God's answer to your prayer, whether it's "yes," "no," or "not right now."

ONE FINAL THOUGHT

·When you're in pain, God's answer to your suffering may not always be immediate relief, but you can trust it will always be for your best.

TIMELESS WISDOM FOR EVERYDAY LIVING

On the Edge

God is working in you to make you willing and able to obey him. Philippians 2:13 CEV

The sufferings we have now are nothing compared to the great glory that will be shown us.

Romans 8:18 NCV

You have been given not only the privilege of trusting in Christ but also the privilege of suffering for him.

Philippians 1:29 NLT

Adversity is the diamond dust Heaven polishes its jewels with.

Robert Leighton

Those who suffer because it is God's will for them, should by their good actions trust themselves completely to their Creator, who always keeps his promise.

1 Peter 4:19 GNT

While he lived on earth, anticipating death, Jesus cried out in pain and wept in sorrow as he offered up priestly prayers to God. Because he honored God, God answered him. Though he was God's Son, he learned trusting-obedience by what he suffered, just as we do.

Hebrews 5:7–8 THE MESSAGE

A Christian is someone who shares the sufferings of God in the world.

Dietrich Bonhoeffer

If we had no winter, the spring would not be so pleasant; if we did not sometimes taste of adversity, prosperity would not be so welcome.

Anne Bradstreet

Afflictions are but the shadow of God's wings. George MacDonald

Always and Forever

Jesus said, "Be sure
of this: I am with
you always, even to
the end of the age."
MATTHEW 28:20b NLT

THE STORY BEHIND WHAT JESUS SAID

For forty days after Jesus' death, he appeared to his followers.
Now it was time for Jesus to return to heaven. On a mountain
outside Galilee, the eleven remaining disciples gathered to
hear Jesus' farewell address.

His final words were not "good-bye" but "I am always with
you." The word Jesus used for *always* meant "the whole of
every day." Not a second of the future would pass without
God's Spirit being present in the disciples' lives. Until the day
when Jesus would physically return to judge the earth, his
power would work through the disciples—and all those who
would later choose to follow him. Through life, death, and
beyond, God's Spirit would never leave their side.

REFLECTIONS ON THE WORDS OF JESUS

Your teenage years are a turning point. You leave childhood behind and get your first taste of the freedom and responsibility of adulthood. Big changes lie ahead of you as you consider decisions that will change the course of your future.

The decision that will have the biggest impact on what lies ahead is deciding whom you're going to follow. Choosing to follow God assures you of an amazing future. It allows the power of God's Spirit to work through you, helping you accomplish more than you ever could on your own. It invites the guidance of God's Spirit to lead you boldly through every circumstance. It lets you enjoy the continual presence of God's Spirit as your destiny unfolds moment by moment.

Your decision also determines your future home. Your present relationship with God is just a glimpse of what's to come. One day you'll have the chance to do what the disciples did—see him face-to-face.

ONE FINAL THOUGHT

God's Spirit is continually working within you to draw you closer to God, closer to whom God created you to be, and closer to your true home in heaven.

TIMELESS WISDOM FOR EVERYDAY LIVING

Always and Forever

It's in Christ that we find out who we are and what we are living for. Ephesians 1:11a THE MESSAGE

Jesus has gone to prepare a place for us, and the Holy Spirit has been sent to prepare us for that place.

Author Unknown

I know the plans I have for you, says the Lord. They are plans for good and not for evil, to give you a future and a hope. Jeremiah 29:11 TLB

Never be afraid to trust an unknown future to a known God.

Corrie ten Boom

Since you are God's children, God sent the Spirit of his Son into your hearts.
Galatians 4:6a NCV

Don't let anyone think less of you because you are young. Be an example to all believers in what you teach, in the way you live, in your love, your faith, and your purity.

1 Timothy 4:12 NLT

Reach up as far as you can, and God will reach down all the way.
Bishop Vincent

Let reverence for the LORD be the concern of your life. If it is, you have a bright future.
Proverbs 23:17 GNT

The future is as bright as the promises of God. Adoniram Judson